If only
I'd Known!

If only
I'd Known!

Bernard Carter

This edition published in Great Britain in 2013 by DB Publishing, an imprint of JMD Media.

ISBN 9781780913018

Printed and bound by Copytech (UK) Limited, Peterborough.

Contents

To
The Adventure that is Life

Acknowledgements

Once again I find myself on my knees pleading feebly for clemency from the characters that appear on the pages of this book. Most manifest themselves under a thinly disguised pseudonym, while the remainder have passed on and consequently are in no position to object. Alongside this pathetic plea I wish to express my gratitude to the one living Uncle George who furnished me with past family information. I also wish to include my good friend Archie for his 'Gilbertisation' of the St Andrew dialogue and who, luckily for me lives north of Hadrian's Wall and well out of harm's way. Lastly, my thanks go to my sister Sylvia whose real name is…er…Sylvia, for her contribution to a Saturday night in the 60s. Yet despite all the years that have passed she still refuses to come clean about the amorous 'drain-pipe incident' which I guess will never be made public.

I very much hope this book will revive nostalgia and memories for many, unless of course you can barely remember what you had for breakfast this morning, in which case you will probably not have a clue what I am talking about!

Bernard F. Carter

Introduction

This book more or less picks up from where *'It wasn't Me, Sir!'* left off and although manhood lurked just around the next corner I still found myself just as confused about the rigours of life as I ever did. Strange, mysterious things took place, like my squeaky voice became deep and manly, hairs sprouted in odd places like a recently seeded lawn, and as the sap rose in my veins I felt uneasy. I felt I should be doing something with myself that should involve a girl, but I was not totally certain about just what that something ought to be. My mates naturally took the lead by giving lurid accounts of alleged encounters with Jaqueline Allcock in a field near the tadpole pond. The truth is they were only relating what their big brothers had told them; who really had indulged in carnal delights with Jaqueline Allcock in a field near the tadpole pond! It was quite obvious there was a kind of mental list of 'things to see' on a girl's body which were never fully on show in the pages of the *Reveille Magazine* or *Tit-Bits*.

Having to work for a living and pay my mother for my 'keep' came as a bit of a shock and greatly interrupted my previous freedom. However, it did put money in my pocket and allow me to carve another notch on the staff of life on my way to manhood, for it meant I could buy rounds of drinks in a pub and along with my mates become boisterous, silly and downright paralytic. Of course for me this was just a passing phase, whereas for some people it never passes and they embark upon a career as a raging alcoholic. Another contributory factor was the sobering influence of becoming a married man, where my hard-earned pennies were destined to be spent on humdrum things like parquet flooring tiles, woodchip paper and copious amounts of magnolia and white emulsion paint.

The demands of transportation forced me to sell my trusty bicycle and watch it ride off into the sunset with a stranger in the saddle. I joined the Lambretta scooter brigade and travelled thousands of miles, and with a tank full of Esso I could ride safe in the knowledge that I had 'Put a Tiger in my Tank' and I even had the ubiquitous furry nylon tiger-tail hanging from the back of the scooter as undeniable proof. Life became hectic as I tried to spread my time between being a married man, a full-time photographic student, falling from rock faces and squirming down muddy holes in the ground. All these activities were tenuously linked by plenteous amounts of Watney's Red Barrel and a general attitude that life was not to be taken too seriously. The latter in itself became quite challenging when I got my first responsible job as Head Photographer (Okay, I'll come clean, there was only me in the department, but it sounded important.) at a research station in East Anglia that was overrun by eccentric boffins and deadly earnest, poker-faced doctors in white coats. This really was serious stuff and I felt like a square peg in a round hole.

I took my first trip to foreign parts which rammed home the fact that the French are in fact quite different to us, and how I wished I had paid more attention to the language lessons at school. Asking for a croissant is one thing, but being totally unaware and a little surprised that my rectum was about to be spiked by a thermometer in the hands of an abrasive 'docteur' is quite another matter altogether.

Being young and with many of life's most onerous situations yet to come it was all too easy to be egotistical and cocky as generations before me and after me will testify. We thought parents and oldies were square, un-cool, out of touch and unable to get with the beat. We were youthful, indestructible and thought we knew it all, especially one of my uncle Georges who really did think he knew it all and was in the habit of constantly reminding us of this fact, or put another way, delusion. From here on in my life took many unexpected twists and turns, but despite this it was, and still is as it should always be… a perpetual adventure.

'Sticky Willy, Anyone?'

I think it is fairly safe to say that the opportunity of seeing a body draped over the top of the pyramidal metal roof of an electricity sub-station has to be very rare indeed. But such an event did occur and I personally witnessed it on the evening of 4 May 1964, being the owner of said body at the time and well aware of the electrical hum of instant death coming from beneath me. I remember the precise date because it was my nineteenth birthday and I had been out celebrating with Al, a friend from work and my climbing partner Kev. I had already successfully scaled a pillar box that night with its obliging postal slot foothold, but had failed badly on an ascent of a telephone booth, due no doubt to several pints of Watney's Red Barrel that had rendered me totally unable to get a grip on either the booth or myself. However, the challenge of the sub-station had been an overwhelming success, but quickly let down by discovering that there was nothing to do up on the roof apart from stagger to my feet, raise both arms in the air and shout, 'I did it because it was there', whereupon I lost my balance and crashed to the ground. These smooth sided steel boxes were dotted about the Chaddesden estate in Derby and because of the nature of their structure had always been seen as a challenge. As kids they appeared to be much bigger, but grubby sticky hands helped us to get a good purchase on the metal to hoist ourselves up onto the roof. Sticky hands, which we possessed most of the time gave us the climbing abilities on smooth surfaces of an Amazonian tree frog which is more than capable of climbing up a pane of glass, not that there are many of those in the south American rainforest. I offer this snippet of 'guaranteed to break the icy silence at any dinner party' information because I once kept green tree frogs as pets and they could scale the windows and wallpaper at home with ease. In fact one even scaled the awesome overhang of my grannies bosom, which in 'froggy' terms would be the equivalent of tackling Kilnsey Crag overhang in Yorkshire. It caused granny much amusement until 'froggy' reached the neckline of her frock and headed into the forbidden territory of her formidable cleavage. This was one very brave frog for I doubt that even my grandfather, who had come unscathed through both the Somme and Passchendaele had dared to tackle granny's cleavage for many years. Undaunted, 'froggy' continued his exploration despite granny now flailing her arms around in a mild fit of hysterics and yelling at my father, 'George! George! Get this thing off me.' My father was only really interested in reading the next page of his library book, so my mother bounded to the rescue and diffused the situation. Once released 'froggy' scrambled up the wall to the picture rail where he puffed out his throat and made a noise not unlike someone blowing a raspberry. He was definitely a frog with attitude.

Anyway, back to the night of my birthday. After a lot of drunken silliness, Al and Kev picked me up off the ground and delivered me home. As it was a Monday, this meant I had to sober-up for work the following day and be in complete control of my bicycle which might prove difficult. Having a birthday on a Monday was seriously bad planning, whereas my actual day of birth was a Friday thus enabling me to have the entire weekend to look forward to, though naturally having only just been born I had not really arranged anything special beyond eating and filling my nappy with something quite objectionable. I had been in full-time employment since February the previous year after finally leaving the Joseph Wright School of Art. This came about by a handful of mates and me having been encouraged by the headmaster to leave which was really tantamount to eviction. He strongly implied that we were doing very little and taking up useful space in his school. He forced us into finding a job. We were more than happy to do very little and take up valuable space in his classrooms, but it was not to be.

I began work as an Assistant Technician for the Derbyshire Schools Museum Service which was just up from Five Lamps on Duffield Road. It was a grand old building set back from the road with a short driveway and within its interior I had to learn for the first time about life without my peers and acquire the skills of museum presentation. Basically the educational needs of schools throughout the county of Derbyshire were supplemented by us providing them with exhibits on history, geography, geology, art, music and film. The department I worked in dealt with the first four subjects. The film library was in a downstairs room and the records were in another room upstairs near my department. It was the sole responsibility of a young girl with a very loud 'plummy' voice whose participation in amateur dramatics was apparent on a daily basis. Although her room was some distance from us, her devotion to Gilbert and Sullivan could often prove painful, irritating and fostered an overwhelming desire to either smash the record or strangle her, whichever was the more convenient option. My two work colleagues were as different as 'chalk and cheese'. One being a young, flirtatious married woman called Beth, while our immediate boss Paul, who was a decent tolerant chap had proclivities that lay favourably towards the male genre. One of the first things he taught me, after I had first donned a white laboratory coat to at least make me look professional was how to set-up and operate a hand press for printing labels for the exhibits. However, having once been a 'whizz-kid' with a John Bull printing outfit laying type out back-to-front came easily to me. Even now I can write back-to-front, but find in general that people quickly lose interest reading their Christmas cards if they have to use a mirror.

Exhibits were normally housed in ordinary brown suitcases or specially made boxes with sheet polystyrene interiors cut to hold the contents. For example, a history case on Egypt might contain objects from an ancient tomb. These would be set in polystyrene with finger cavities to enable the objects to be taken out for everything was geared towards being a 'hands on' experience for the children, which predictably had its downside. Cutting out the shapes was usually my job and I had the unenviable task of grappling with a sheet of polystyrene on a foot-treadle operated fretsaw. This created a terrible mess of static-sticking polystyrene balls which adhered to everything but mainly to me. After a session of this I would emerge looking like I had just come inside from a snow blizzard and could very easily have triggered a rumour that Captain Oates of, 'I am just going outside and may be some time' fame was in fact alive and well having been spotted years later in the vicinity of Duffield Road. An alternative method of cutting out shapes was by using a lethal electrical device which would have sent a present day health and safety inspector into an advanced state of apoplexy. From a wall plug emerged two wires that were connected to each end of a stouter wire by the use of two porcelain connector blocks. When switched on the wire glowed red-hot and after first being threaded through the polystyrene it was nervously guided to melt its way around the required shape. This meant holding the hot wire taught by the two connectors which continually threatened to burn my finger ends as I choked in the toxic smoke and fumes of melting polystyrene. Nobody even considered the use of protective gloves, goggles or a breathing mask. I wonder if it had been sanctioned by our own electrician who worked in another building on Kedleston Road. Strange though it may seem, and it is strange, this man turned out to be colour-blind.

"How do you know which wire does what?" I once asked him.

"Simple" he replied, "I just trace them back to their source."

This must have been a time-consuming process and I wondered whether he was in the right job. Imagine if he had been a member of a bomb disposal squad.

"Now which of these wires shall I cut? They all look grey to me. Perhaps if I just pull this one gently and see what its attached t"... Flash... BOOM!!

The entire hot-wire thing was so crude it would probably have been best suited to the needs of a merciless interrogator in some despot ruled country. It is little wonder that in later life I did not develop polystyrene cutters lung! Of course it did not stop there for I was sometimes required to use neat sulphuric acid on metal objects fully aware that any accidental spillage over my feet could result in me cycling home with raw stumps stuck to my pedals. It was not a chemical to be messed with.

The 'hands on' policy normally meant that many objects had to be cleaned upon their return and it was sometimes quite incredible to realise for example, that some funerary figure that had lain in a tomb since 1450 bc now bore the greasy finger prints of a schoolchild who had obviously had fish paste sandwiches for lunch, which on reflection would have been more beneficial to a Pharoah on his journey to an afterlife than a useless pottery figure. Another time a couple of Roman pottery oil lamps came back with large holes in their bases. This had been caused by some little 'darling' (for darling read clumsy-handed half-witted child who should have been dealt a smack around the head) who had poked a finger through each one, thus rendering them utterly useless and not even fit for me to take home as back-up during a power failure. However, when the plaster replica of the well-known *Queen of Benin* bronze arrived from loan smashed to a jigsaw puzzle of pieces, I did take that home. I spent hours piecing it back together and despite being broken a second time by some cack-handed burglar she now sits serenely on a shelf in my upstairs lavatory. Not I hasten to add through lack of respect, but through lack of space and it is only the necessity of nature that causes me to drop my trousers and momentarily do a 'moonie' in front of this one-time figure of African royalty.

Every work morning was hell for me. The first job of the day was among the vast collection of framed prints of paintings by the great and the glorious that had hung on the classroom walls for several weeks gathering layers of dust. Now dust and I are life-long enemies. As a child I suffered from the condition called hay fever, which does not necessarily relate to hay, but I spent a lot on time on my back on my bed sneezing, snuffling and downing Piriton tablets like Smarties along with pumping decongestant sprays up both nostrils like there was no tomorrow. My eyes would stream constantly and so would my nose, and the continued use of handkerchiefs and tissues made it red, raw and throbbing as my misery was exacerbated by outburst of agonising 'blind spots' that sprung up on my nose like molehills on a lawn. Wiping my nose and wiping my eyes forced me to endure blinding, searing pain for days, especially during the summer months. In an attempt to get to the bottom of all this I decided to have my sinuses drained. I and three other victims firstly had our sinuses desensitised with a wad of cotton wool soaked in some ghastly concoction that was then thrust up our nostrils on the end of a ridiculously long wire. Waiting for it to take effect we sat in a row on a bench in a waiting room hunched forward with long wires protruding from our nostrils like a quartet of insects with misplaced feelers. We were silent and forlorn as we tuned in to the screaming of a patient who had gone in before us. Apparently he had had his sinuses punctured before so the nurse told him he did not require anesthetizing. The screams suggested otherwise. After the whole grisly procedure of hearing my own inner nostril being crunched as the nurse battered her way in like a team of navvies digging out the channel tunnel, a few hours later I regained my usual blocked nose and continued to sneeze. It really had been an utter waste of time. 'If only I'd known' I muttered to myself. Now you will understand why dust and I formed an unhappy relationship and cleaning dusty picture frames transformed my mornings into a living nightmare. I sneezed over Van Gogh's *Sunflowers*. I sneezed over Constable's *The Haywain*, and I sneezed over Landseer's *Monarch of the Glen*. In truth I sneezed over the best of them which in turn required even more cleaning!

Al, from work who became a good friend was an assistant to an older man who drove the museum van around the county delivering and collecting from the schools. Prior to this, Al had been employed in the building industry, but after having an accident at a power station site he rather lost interest. It seems he had tripped over something and fell on the edge of a pit, caught his lower jaw and instantly removed most of his teeth. As he got to his feet with blood and fragments of teeth spilling from his mouth looking like Count Dracula after a particularly messy eating session, it struck him that a career change might be a good move. Still, looking on the bright side, he did get a splendid set of false teeth out of it! The other person I befriended was a girl who worked in the office called Maggie. She was a pleasant looking girl with a lovely personality and a magnificent pair of legs and I took a fancy to her, legs and all. Sadly our paths did not seem to cross very often at work, so I rectified this by seeing her in the kitchen where she made the office tea twice a day. I used the kitchen for washing out paint brushes so I would slope off at tea making time on the pretence of washing out my endless supply of dirty brushes. In my naivety I thought I was being quite nonchalant about the whole thing, whereas in truth my predictable disappearances made me look a complete clown which caused unprecedented outbursts of sniggering and tittering from my two colleagues. It looked like true love was never going to have a chance for the other obstacle in our path was the fact that Maggie lived in Crich. Now that is a fair cycle ride of an evening with an absolute killer of a hill up to the village. In all probability any anticipated kiss I thought I might get would, as likely as not, be the kiss of life from an over-zealous member of the local St John Ambulance with a hairy face and chronic halitosis. I am not referring to a bearded man either. Although that comment sounds a little harsh, I did in fact once know someone who fitted the bill. She did have a severe breath problem and despite her training and loyalty to the 'calling' she always maintained that she could never give anyone the kiss of life especially if the patient was dribbling from the corner of their mouth because the thought of it made her shudder. In fact she never really liked proper kissing much even if she fancied the person. Given this outlook along with her breathy problem it is difficult to assess the benefit or otherwise from the point of view of a dying person in the event of a 'breathy' stand-off. Anyway, the bottom line is that true love never really got off the ground with me and Maggie and I found myself washing out a lot less paint brushes. The odds were heavily stacked against us. Many years later I looked Maggie up where I knew she was working in Belper and took her for dinner at the New Bath Hotel. I did, after waiting all those years finally get a kiss from her when I dropped her home, but I never saw her again. If I remember correctly, she still had a fine pair of legs.

Then a real-life trauma came along that took me by complete surprise. It was the occasion of my first birthday at work. It was Beth who first hit me with it.

"Your birthday tomorrow, isn't it?" she announced across the room at me.

"Yes" I replied innocently.

"Looking forward to the birthday cakes?" she asked, curling her tongue around her lips.

"I don't think I'll be getting a birthday cake" I replied, trying to sound grown up about it all. "Those days are long gone."

"No, no" she carried on, "the cakes for here, you know, for your birthday."

"What cakes?" I queried becoming a tad confused.

"You know" she grinned, "the ones you have to buy everyone at work."

"What, nobody told me anything about that" I answered, feeling a little hot under the collar.

"Oh, yes" she enthused, "It's a tradition that on your birthday you have to treat everyone at work to fresh cream cakes."

I gulped, felt suddenly unwell and turned red in the face. Fresh cream cakes were just too much for me to take in. I never had fresh cream cakes at home. We could not afford such luxuries and anyway my father detested them saying the cream tasted like cart grease. Quite how he knew this is something to be wondered at! He also said those individual rectangular sponge cakes coated in chocolate with tiny bits of chocolate sprinkled over them were questionable on account that to his mind they looked suspiciously like mouse droppings.

"Fresh cream cakes for everyone?" I stammered.

"Yes" she replied, obviously enjoying my dismayed reaction to all this. "I can't wait for mine."

I sunk into instant depression. There were fourteen members of staff. That was fourteen fresh cream cakes to buy including one for myself. It was going to cost me a fortune, and on my meagre earnings? I would be penniless for months and months. I would have to sell my trusty bike. My mother might refuse to feed me and throw me out on the street because I could not pay her my house-keeping money. I would become destitute, starve and probably die beneath the privet hedge of some ones front garden. What a tragic fate people would say. He had such a promising career. Yes indeed, they would say, he was so talented. He was destined for greatness there was never any doubt about that. What an ignominious fate all because of some fresh cream cakes. I mean, it was not as if I liked everyone at work, so why should I have to buy them cakes? I cycled home that evening feeling very dejected and went to bed early. The only way out of this as far as I could see was to hang myself from the light fitting with my pyjama cord. But then I had to face the fact that the fitting would in all likelihood come away from the ceiling bringing down masses of plaster, at which point my father would enter the scene, get very angry about the mess and tell me in no uncertain terms that I had to pay for the damage. I guess I must have fallen asleep for when I awoke it was already 'fresh cream cake' day and I knew I was just going to have to go through with it. That lunchtime I was allowed out early from work so I could walk into town to buy the cakes. I selected some cream horns, chocolate eclairs, cream puffs, cream doughnuts and some cream filled, pink iced fingers.

On the subject of iced fingers, my wife informs me that as a young girl attending the historical Battle Abbey all-girls school whose grounds include the site of 1066 where a stray arrow took out Harold's eye, thus rendering him far beyond the help of anything that Specsavers might come up with, iced fingers were always known as 'sticky willies'. These were an absolute must on the menu when a midnight feast in the dormitory was being planned and there is little doubt that the mention of 'sticky willies' sparked off a round of girly tittering. Picture the scene of a giggling gaggle of innocent, virginal, blossoming young schoolgirls grouped around a plate of pink iced fingers.

"I say, Phoebe old thing, care for a sticky willy?" piped up Nicola in her high, cut-glass voice.

"Oh rather, absolutely adore the things" replied a drooling Phoebe, who with wide-eyed enthusiasm eagerly rammed a sticky willy into her mouth, rolling her eyes in pleasure and licking some stray cream off her fingers with the decorum that befits a private schoolgirl.

"Anyone else for a sticky willy?" at which point a tangle of arms and grasping hands shot forward as sticky willies flew off the plate quicker than you could shake a stick at a dog in an effort to sate those schoolgirl fantasies.

I fear however, and I think it only right that I should say this, that in my opinion anyone who has a willy, sticky or otherwise that closely resembles a pink iced finger with fresh cream needs to seek immediate medical attention.

Armed with three boxes of cakes and an empty wallet I trudged back to work. During afternoon tea I watched them all being devoured in front of me accompanied by a tuneless rendition of *Happy Birthday*. At least it effectively drowned out the sound of me muttering to myself through a fixed grin. I wish I had lied about my birth date claiming I was born on 29 February which at least would have given me three years to save up for those damned fresh cream cakes. I cannot account for this, but shortly after the life-scarring cream cake incident I took to smoking a pipe! I started out with one of those long-stemmed, sticky-out pipes but found it always seemed to be in the way when opening a door, or trying to pull on a sweater, so I graduated onto a curled chin warmer which suited me better. The strange thing about smoking is that when for example, you smoke your first cigarette which in my case would have been a covert underage gasp on a Park Drive or Woodbine, the immediate effect it has on you is to make you a bit light-headed followed by an almost uncontrollable desire to empty the contents of your stomach on the floor of the telephone booth where underage pioneer smokers tended to gather. Smoke a pipe and you enter a whole new social spectrum associated with intelligentsia, academia and sagacity, at least on the surface. Obviously if you have always been a moronic, half-baked imbecile then this is not going to wash. The other notable effect that smoking a pipe has is the way it scorches the lining of your mouth causing considerable discomfort to the point where you have to seriously consider the merits of an open mouth and a fire extinguisher. Holland House was a sweet-tasting fragrant tobacco that I favoured as a beginner, but later moved onto the more rugged Voortrekker. I felt it made me more strapping and manly to smoke this as the Voortrekkers, a bunch of Dutch farming pioneers and grossly outnumbered, had given twelve thousand of those Zulu chappies a damned good thrashing at Blood River in South Africa. This happened on 16 December, 1838 and I bet a lot of celebratory pipe smoking went off that night and well into Christmas! There used to be a wonderful tobacconist near the bottom of Green Lane that catered for every smokers need and it was there that I bought my first pipe, pipe cleaners and most importantly, a pipe-smokers tool. This consisted of a fold away gadget comprising of a reamer, a prodder and a tamper which regardless of them sounding like questionable professions in the sex industry were in reality indispensable to an avid pipe smoker. I felt I had now mastered one step towards manhood and maturity, which left me with the other rite of passage that was easily available (so that excludes sex from the equation) which was the demon drink.

Plastered for Christmas

The thing about adolescence is that it is such a grey area and it is normally unclear as to when you leave it behind and become mature. Some people of course never successfully achieve the transition, but the majority of us do make an effort. The metamorphosis from childhood to adolescence is definitely noticeable because of certain events happening most of which nature has laid on for us. For me it was the fact that I could now wear long trousers, speak without sounding as though I had trapped something vital in the hinges of a door and becoming aware of strong sensations which accompanied the sap of youth rising in my veins. These events alone (well maybe not the long trousers) and to use the common vernacular that signified somewhat crudely that in fact my 'balls' had dropped meant I was on the right track. It can prove to be a worrying description if the ball dropping event has yet to take place. It left me wondering through ignorance if I should take it literally and unexpectedly discover they had detached themselves overnight and find them the following morning at the bottom of my bed stuck to the woolly cover of a cold water bottle. If it was planned to happen during the day, would I find them lodged in the top of my socks leaving me with the embarrassing dilemma of how to dispose of them; and would they make a noise when they dropped? It was the not knowing that gave me sleepless nights and kept me in a state of anxiety.

This particular process of change seemed to usher in what is best described as a pheromonal odour around that specific area of my trousers and inducing a degree of paranoia for I was convinced that everyone could smell me. I felt sure everyone on the bus could smell me. Everyone in a shop could smell me apart from in the local fish and chip shop where I could temporarily relax as the aroma of fish and chips outdoes most other pongs lingering in the air. I quickly realised there was a limit to just how long I could loiter in a fish and chip shop without buying anything. The alternative would be to gorge myself hour after hour on fish, chips and mushy peas, become grossly obese and die at an early age of a heart attack. Puberty, who needs it? It really all came to the forefront one evening when sitting on the sofa alongside Linsey's parents making small talk with my legs firmly crossed. Linsey had been a sort of one-time girl-friend who worked at the Greyhound track, but she seemed to lavish more affection on the racing dogs than on me. As so often happens in life, she has gone, her house has gone and so indeed has the dog track. Stylish accommodation now occupies the site where originally criminals, felons and murderers formerly languished in cells with the occasional one being hauled outside now and then for a bit of fresh air, a leg stretch and a very permanent neck stretch much to the delight and entertainment of a gathered crowd of merry-makers. Yet people still to this day ask what did generations before us do to amuse themselves before the advent of television? Ipso facto! Anyway, back on the sofa I found myself in an awkward predicament trying to fend off their dog Rex who was determined to thrust his snuffling face into my crotch with all the gusto of a dog digging for a bone.

"He's certainly taken a fancy to you" smiled Linsey's mum. "He's not normally very good with strangers. Would you like another cup of tea love?" she beamed. What I really wanted to do was disappear down the back of the sofa. Over-excited Rex was getting out of control and not because he liked me!

"Here, have a slice of cherry Madeira" she insisted. "Mind you don't drop any crumbs or Rex will be in like a shot."

The thing is Rex was already in like a shot and continued to pester me in a state of (Rex, not me) semi-arousal. Finally, and much to my relief Linsey's dad hauled the dog off and pushed the reluctant Rex into the backyard where he whined piteously until Linsey's dad yelled at him and gave him a smart smack across his head, whereupon all went quiet. "I think we should all go down the road and have a drink" he suggested, which we all did, apart from Rex of course who did not deserve one. What he did deserve was a bucket of cold water thrown over him.

Other changes occurred as adulthood warily reared its head and hitherto naked parts of my body began to sprout hair and I wondered why? Facial fluff turned into hair and had to be dealt with on a daily basis by clumsily hacking at it with an ancient Wilkinson razor which my father said I could use. It had resided in the bathroom cabinet for umpteen years looking anodised and not much use for anything, which is precisely what I discovered in a very short space of time. Consequently early shaving sessions saw me emerging from the bathroom having chopped lumps out of my face and skimmed the head of a few spots and covered with enough bloodied pieces of lavatory paper to give the impression that I had had a very close encounter with an exploding toilet roll. There were more revolutionary changes such as washing daily, cleaning my teeth daily, changing my underpants more than once a week, using Brilliantine on my hair (did you know that the French version of the film *Grease* was called *Brilliantine*?... yeah, wha'ever…) and becoming moody, objectionable and stroppy. The latter being an age-old problem and every parent's nightmare that causes many to question their earlier decision to start a family, throw their hands up in despair and unanimously lament 'Why didn't somebody tell us?' Suddenly, keeping goldfish becomes a belated, but nevertheless, an increasingly attractive alternative.

The real milestone on the road to maturity, giving you misplaced credibility among your peers is being able to walk into a pub and order your first round of drinks and settle in with other drinkers, blindly unaware of just where this is going to lead you. My first steps into the ruinous world of alcohol came when I along with Al and Kev first entered the portal of the Osmaston Park Hotel and downed our first couple of bottles of Mackeson. It would take time for my palette to accept the bitterness of real beer. This pub was the other side of town from where I lived and entailed a cycle ride down Nottingham road, then the entire length of Raynesway and beyond, but this seemed to be of no consequence at the time. The truth is there was a pub just around the corner from where I lived which even had its own 'off-licence', but it was a newish estate pub and devoid of either charm or character. I only ever went in it once and that was enough. It had the air of a cell for the condemned about it and the inmates propping up the bar smoking and swearing would probably have fared quite well in Alcatraz. For reasons I have never been able to fathom it was called The Rhino. Now you have to admit that with the best will in the world it would require downing a fair quantity of beer to even begin to imagine you had seen one of these beasts wandering the streets of Chaddesden! The pub even sported rather bizarrely, the head of a real Rhino fixed to the wall of an outside shelter. It deteriorated over the years and finally disappeared as indeed have the customers for the pub for it is now boarded up and abandoned. However, I have come to the conclusion that the pub was never given its full name The Rhinoceros because of the pronunciation problems it would have caused when you had had more than a skin-full and found yourself confronted by an irate wife.

"And what time do you call this? Three hours ago I sent you out for twenty Players, three hours ago!"

"I'msh shorry luv, I…"

"Don't sorry me. Where the hell have you been?"

"I had a fuwsh beers at the Rhinoshterus."

"What?"

"The Rhinosher…..nosterosh."

"Oh for heaven's sake get up the stairs you drunken useless article."

It seems an extraordinary name to give a pub given its location, but then again names often make little sense.

The street names for example, where I lived made sense to a degree because they were named after towns or counties, so Ripon Crescent, Worcester Crescent, Winchester Crescent, (once the capital of England, Winchester that is not the crescent) Perth Street, Wiltshire Road were logically acceptable until suddenly in the middle of all this you come across Max Road. To me Max Road sounds like an aging comedian that Leonard Sachs had revived for 'one night only ladies and gentlemen' at the Leeds City Variety Hall. 'We now have for your amusement and titillation the master of mirth, the maestro of merriment and madcap mayhem, the one, the only Maaaaaaaax Road!!' But then it becomes even more puzzling when the road slicing through all the Crescents is called St Andrew's View. Now where did that spring from? On the surface it would seem unlikely that St Andrew himself, the Patron Saint of Scotland ever stood on top of the hill behind Roe Farm School gazing out over the dubious wonders of Chaddesden and beyond. Then again, anything is possible.

"Oh, it's a fine view is that Jimmy. Do you know I can see all the way to yon cooling towers at Willington."

"Yi tell me that" replied a disinterested Jimmy, who was noisily engaged in munching his way through a cold haggis sandwich. Jimmy was St Andrew's sidekick for obviously a cultured, learned saint required an underling to carry the sandwiches, a flask of tea and the necessary assortment of quick change, all weather halos.

"Maybe I'll call it St Andrew's View. What do you think Jimmy?"

"Oh aye, that's a richt braw name" muttered Jimmy. "Folk'll no forget a name like that in a hurry."

"Then St Andrew's View it is. Now I don't know about you Jimmy, but I think it's time we headed back home as I'm feeling a bit peckish and could do with a bite to eat."

"Dinny fash yousel' about eatin' Andra" enthused Jimmy. "Ma guid wife'll nae dout hae a muckle sheep's heed hotterin' on the ingle and yir favourite for efters."

"Oh! You dinny mean a clootie dumpling?" drooled St Andrew, wiping the corner of his mouth on the cuff of his saintly sleeve.

"As sure's you're leevin Andra."

"Well" pronounced St Andrew. "What man as could call himself a man wouldn't walk the length of England just to sink his teeth into one of your wife's dumplings? But there is just one more thing" he continued, turning on Jimmy and fixing him with a penetrating stare.

"And whit wid that be Andra?" enquired Jimmy, picking out a stringy piece of haggis from between his teeth.

"DON'T CALL ME ANDRA!! You disrespectful little piece of s… God in heaven, you'd try the patience of a saint!"

And so the pair of them wandered back to Scotland bickering about who had drunk the last of the tea. But from that day on, St Andrew's View it became.

Okay, so I hold my hand up to knowing that legend has it St Andrew back in Greece, had a bit of a 'to-do' with the Romans who decided to teach him a lesson by pinning him to a cross for being a bit too lippy. This was all a very long time ago, yet somehow a few of the Saint's bones assisted by the then equivalent of Parcel Force, found their way to the shores of Scotland at a place called, and here there must have been a lot of head scratching and pacing up and down the foreshore before someone came up with the brilliant name, St Andrews. I think my version of events is more interesting and just to prove that I have exhausted all possibilities for the naming of St Andrews View, it should be considered that on a clear day, with truly exceptional eye sight it was once possible to spot St Andrews on the coast of Fife from the top of the hill behind Roe Farm School. I use the word 'was' because this miracle could only have taken place before Taylor Wimpey came along and ruined the view by erecting an estate of 'flat-pack' houses. They were lifted I recall, a side at a time by a crane and then fixed together with nuts and bolts. The entire operation brought to mind those Bayko plastic construction kits of walls, window frames, doors and a roof that could be bought in the nineteen fifties and early sixties. Well, I think I have thoroughly exhausted the subject and also myself to the extent that I no longer have the will, or the energy to contemplate the connotations behind the naming of Sussex Circus!

Meanwhile back to the matter of drink, the pursuit of which quickly became, as it tends to, a weekly event and having finally ventured into the world of real beer and an occasional whisky I was well on the way to ruin, especially financial ruin. This was despite having change from a pound note after ordering three pints of beer. The real testing ground is of course Christmas, and what would Christmas be without getting totally drunk, wrecked, plastered, gassed, sloshed, wasted, paralytic, ratted, and for the cultured, Brahms and Liszt to mention just a few of the descriptions given to the state of inebriation. At work this meant an extended lunch break so everyone could tramp down the road to the Seven Stars and have a drink or two (if only that had been the case) to celebrate Christmas. For me and Al this would be an excuse for a drinking competition to see which of us was the most macho, or put another way the most pea-brained of the pair of us. After downing several pints of beer along with several trips to the lavatory, which is where most beer ends up or outside on the pavement, we decided to hit the whisky. And so it went on round after round after round, until at the sixteenth tot a voice came through the muggy haze announcing it was time to get back to work, not that anyone had any intention of doing any because there was Christmas afternoon tea waiting for us all. Everyone filed out of the pub and began to drift back up the road except for me and Al who being the worse for wear found we were able to drift everywhere apart from in the right direction. After staggering into the road a few times to wave and burble a 'Merry Chrishmush' at passing motorists, then colliding with a lamp-post which did nothing for the already addled condition of our brains, we miraculously made it back to work. Paul who had stayed behind not wishing to be a part of the drinking looked none too pleased at the state we were in. Everyone else seemed to find it quite entertaining. We all assembled in the staff tea-room where I was confronted by a table laid out with sausage rolls, crisps, some of those brown foul-tasting twiggy things that look like the leftovers from a Jackdaws nest and a selection of, yes you guessed it, cream cakes. I viewed the sight through increasing waves of nausea. Everybody stood around chatting about Christmas shopping and other seasonal trivia while I and Al, still competing for the number one spot in the Christmas numbskull competition waded into the fare with forced fervour. After what seemed like an eternity of gorging we were all told that we could leave early and go home. Hats and coats were put on to a background babble of 'Have a good Christmas' and 'Don't burn the turkey.' 'Don't drink too much.' 'Don't do anything I wouldn't do' and other equally imbecilic comments. It gave the impression that Christmas was not to be enjoyed too much and was not an excuse to indulge in any degree of excess be it food, drink and probably sex as well. Although it has to be said that with a stomach close to bursting full of turkey and Christmas pudding, and the mother-in-law insisting that everyone sit down and watch the Queen's speech on the telly, the latter activity is unlikely to be on the agenda anyway. On reflection this is possibly a good thing as a session of alcohol fuelled 'slap and tickle' could finish with an afternoon spent in A&E having pine needles from the

Christmas tree removed from embarrassing or even inaccessible places!

For me the real challenge of the day now was how to get home. I clumsily felt my way along the passage-way to the front door, went outside, missed the step and crashed to the ground. I eventually managed to stagger to my feet and stumble across the yard to where my bicycle was parked against a wall. I stared at it for some time trying desperately to figure out which of the two floating seats was the real one. Actually, for one fleeting moment I could have sworn I saw three! After a considerable amount of determination, concentration and luck I mounted my bicycle, wobbled around in a half circle, hit a wall and fell off. I lay there thinking that things were not really going too well and the world was spinning at an alarming rate and I felt very, very sick. Undaunted, I finally managed to get back into the saddle a second time, career down the drive and straight out onto Duffield Road which as luck would have it was free of traffic, thus enabling me to relate this tale. I zoomed fearlessly past Five Lamps which for some reason had become ten and turned into North Street. My route took me across a footbridge alongside the Great Northern Railway line that spanned the river Derwent. The bottom end of this pathway descended into a gloomy narrow walkway hemmed in by a high factory wall on one side and a high wooden fence on the other. It was here one morning that a man had exposed his 'pink iced finger' at a passing female who was of mature years and had probably seen more than a few 'pink iced-fingers' in her time. Nevertheless, she was a tad put out at the sight so soon after breakfast and reported it to the police. As it had been a particularly frosty morning, in all likelihood it was going to be more a case of 'pink prawn' rather than 'pink iced finger'. Meanwhile, I somehow got to the end of the pathway where it emerged onto Chester Green Road. All around this area of course, history has left its mark proving that legions of Roman soldiers clad in leather skirts and open-toed sandals were once fed and watered here. I too left my mark here, for having been folded double over my drop-handlebars my compressed stomach went into rebellious mode forcing an ill-matched combination of alcohol, sausage roll and cream cake to gush forth as a sort of brown sludge reeking of Bells whisky. Leaning with both hands against the wall of the aptly named Bliss factory I decorated the wall in a manner that in future years would probably have been a fair contender for the Turner Prize. A train roared close by making a detour into one side of my throbbing head and out the other. I felt a little better afterwards and continued along the road weaving unsteadily towards the traffic mayhem of Mansfield Road. On the corner was a shop where a very saucy lady used to sell me chocolate bars and from whom I bought my very first shirt. She sold clothes as well as sweets in case you are wondering. The shop now offers a cleaning and ironing service with a quirky sign inviting you to Drop Your Trousers Here. However, I was in no state for eating chocolate bars, trying on a shirt, or dropping my trousers, so continued my wobbly way successfully running the gauntlet of the heavy traffic and arriving at the bottom of the hill on Hampshire Road. Strangely it seemed to take on the severity of K2 which to my knowledge nobody has ever cycled up. I ascended it by using my bicycle as a kind of Zimmer frame as it was the only thing that stopped me falling over. I fell through the kitchen door at home where my mother announced immediately that dinner was ready. "Phew! You've been drinking" she astutely observed. "You smell like a brewery and have you been sick?" How did she know these things? I forced down a bit of dinner, went to lie down for an hour, changed into my 'going out' clothes and left to catch the bus into town to meet Al and Kev for a Christmas drink, or two, or three. There would be time later on to sober up as I joined the rest of the human wreckage, both girls and lads walking the long walk on Christmas Eve along a deserted Nottingham Road because we had all missed the last bus home.

When I look back I quickly realise that the whole Christmas package, once simple and innocent when a child, goes completely out of the window as you allegedly become mature. It somehow gets swamped in booze, biliousness and thumping hangovers that convince you someone is doing a DIY project on your skull with a power drill. When I was a child Christmas was, along with going on a summer holiday an exciting time and something to be innocently enjoyed. Breaking up at school for the Christmas holidays was always an event celebrated by the classroom party where we all brought in items of food which we particularly liked ourselves, and in the true spirit of Christmas and of giving, we normally scoffed ourselves before anyone else had a chance to with their grubby hands. We would be handed out carol sheets which allowed us to rush out of school and embark upon a money-making career of singing carols outside the neighbourhood front doors. And so it came to pass that the households of Chaddesden were subjected to a cacophony of toe-curling renditions of *Away in a Manger, O Little Town of Bethlehem* and *Oh, Come all Ye Faithful* sung in a continual monotonous drone that was our speciality. If nobody opened the door to us then we would finish off with 'Christmas is coming, the goose is getting fat. Please put a penny in the old man's hat. If you haven't got a penny, a ha'penny will do. And if you haven't got a ha'penny then God bless you' which was a polite way of expressing our feelings towards the occupants that we considered to be too mean to reward us for our efforts. We would then stamp on their garden and kick the gate on our way out. Unless you were able to gulp your tea down at break-neck speed and roar out of the house to embark upon this carol singing spree then you would find that other groups of kids had beaten you to it and Mrs Walker, Mrs Gill, Mrs Stevens and a hundred other mothers throughout the estate would refuse to open their doors to you because they were already sick to the back teeth of Christmas caterwauling. In retrospect this was probably fortuitous as they were, in all probability ready to kill, which might just rob you of your dreams of fame and stardom and the chance to sing in *Christmas Carols from Kings College* on the radio next year. Fat chance!

On the home front there was always a predictable comfort in hanging out year after year the same old coloured crepe-paper garlands strung from the corners of the living room to the central lightshade. Every year the same old bits of tinsel, coloured balls and silver fir cones were strung over the sticky-out branches of the small collapsible Christmas tree that stood on its red wooden block base; and every year the same old plaster Santa suffered the ignominy of having the top of the tree rammed up his nether regions for three weeks every year which would have brought tears to the eyes of the most stoic of Santas. I bet every year my mother took the top of the box of decorations that plaster Santa would grimace and mutter to himself 'Oh no! It's b….y Christmas again, I hate being a Santa. If only I'd known.' But it was the simplicity of it all that proved so endearing, whereas nowadays everyone has epileptic inducing lights strung over everything it is possible to string a line of lights over from the chimney pot down to the hedge of the front garden. Signs pop up saying 'Santa Stop Here' and 'I've Been Good', whereas what they should be saying is 'We've got central heating and no chimney pot. Please leave presents in the front porch.' Just in case Santa should suffer an identity crisis there are plenty of inflatable obese Santas waving about outside the front of houses along with inflatable Snowmen, inflatable Christmas trees and inflatable Reindeer, all of which seem to have been purposely manufactured to self-deflate within a few hours of being pumped up and hang forlornly from a drainpipe or garage roof for the rest of the Christmas period. I recall seeing one recently lying in a semi-deflated state in the driveway of a house. He appeared to have been trying to escape but had collapsed, literally, on the gravel. Lying on his back he looked for all the world as if the run up to Christmas had really been just too much to bear, and the thought of that impending tight schedule of world-wide delivery, astronomical numbers of chimneys to descend, gallons of sherry to swig, an incalculable tonnage of mince pies to eat, plus flying in all weathers with a team of stroppy, hoodlum reindeers had finally pushed him over the edge. He was resigned to his fate and did not seem to be bothered by the fact that it would only be a matter of time before somebody ran over him reversing the car out of the garage. A partially deflated Santa is a memorably sorry sight. I suspect his days are numbered anyway as increasing internet trading means his job will be performed by delivery men in white vans with 'Sign here, please' clipboards or those electronic things that are akin to signing your name on a piece of glass with a twig! And speaking of sorry sights, what about all the poor old turkeys? You do not see them flapping their wings about shouting 'Whoopee! It's nearly Christmas.' Particularly as it nears 25 December and someone lets the cat out of the bag and informs them that they are to be the main attraction on the dinner table, stuffed with sage and onion and ringed with roast potatoes. Suddenly it dawns on those poor grotesque-looking, bald-headed, wattle-swinging gobblers that what until then they had thought were compliments from people saying "Yummy, they look like a juicy pair of thighs' and 'Those full breasts look good enough to eat' were misunderstood. And another thing, they really have no reason to suspect they are so ugly for they have never seen themselves in a mirror and each bird probably thinks it is all the other birds that look so hideous. For most turkeys Christmas is the end of their year as there are very few around to join in a chorus of *Auld Lang Syne*. I wonder if it is because they are so unattractive that they receive so little sympathy and would we feel the same if Christmas dinner was for example, roast cuddly Koala bear? Okay, so there would be no parson's nose, but you see where I am coming from?

The equation of Christmas + drink = embarrassment, is as likely as not something that most of us have experienced and from which some people never seem to learn. Sometimes it dawns on them early on in life, others later in life, but there will always be those who never quite see the utter waste and folly of getting drunk. I remember another Christmas gathering in my early twenties when I was spending time as a guest of a family living on an RAF camp. The party consisted mainly of friends and associates from where I then worked and it was not long before the beer and the spirits were flowing in copious amounts, much of it in the direction of my gullet. After several hours of this and long before the party was over I appeared to be well and truly part of some high speed planetary system from which there was no escape. Obviously I had become an embarrassment and was hauled upstairs by two friends and dumped on a bed. I was ordered to lie on the bed with one leg hanging over the edge touching the ground for this was supposed to be a recommended strategy to eliminate the swirling dizziness that had become my world. As I recall, all it did was make my foot feel as though it had become detached from my leg and was elsewhere in the room. Every now and then someone would enter the room to see if I was still alive and be rewarded by my slurred burbling of just how much I loved everybody including people I had never met. My drunken affections knew no bounds and I would have showered them on anyone who came to my bedside whether it had been Mary Poppins or Vlad the Impaler. I would have told them I loved them all, which in the case of Vlad the Impaler would have been a serious mistake. (Yes, you have spotted an unintended pun there.) The next morning I awoke with a tropical thunderstorm underway inside my head and my kidneys draped over the bed end. Such are the questionable pleasures of the demon drink. Christmas has a lot to answer for and it is an on-going challenge especially when you are young to get through the season relatively unscathed. Office parties of course, are notorious for embarrassing situations. There is nearly always at least one frustrated married woman from accounts who pins you up against a wall, leans her body heavily against yours and in a vaporous cloud of Gin and Tonic fumes asks you if you want to have sex with her, something she will vehemently deny the following day regardless of whether you took her up on the offer or not.

I cannot blame Christmas entirely for drinking in excess. It is simply part of a young hedonistic phase of life regardless of whichever direction it takes, unless you leave school and go straight into a monastery then the pleasures that often accompany drinking will pass you by. Mind you, I cannot help thinking that the order of St Benedict which produces the brandy based liqueur Benedictine, must have had the odd knees-up in the cloisters on a balmy summer evening, their habits held at knee level doing a bit of the old *Hokey Cokey Cokey*. I did not enter a monastery and found that drinking was a deserved necessity after rock climbing and caving which were my main activities when not working. Many Sunday mornings would find me boarding the 'Ramblers train' at Derby Midland station normally with Al and Kev. Al tended to come along just for the banter as Kev was the real climber. He was short in stature with a happy face, curly hair and a pair of wheezing asthmatic lungs which he controlled by the frequent use of an inhaler. I had considered the fact that this could be a disadvantage if, for example, I was leading a climb and Kev was belaying and suddenly he needed both hands to use his inhaler at the very same time as I unintentionally parted company with the rock face. Would I have time to see him just putting the cap back on his inhaler and waving at me shouting, 'Won't be a second' as I plummet past him on the end of a slack rope? We often got off the train at Millers Dale and spent time clambering on the limestone in glorious Water-Cum-Jolly Dale. Looking back I suspect we never took ourselves too seriously knowing we would never be good enough to climb Ravenstor, Malham Cove or the Old Man of Hoy, but we enjoyed our forays into the dales. Often the train journey itself could be a good part of a day out as we might have an encounter. One Sunday it was very crowded on the way back home and we were forced to stand all the way. Fortunately so were a couple of girls who had been out walking for the day and we were soon engaged in conversation. The one I was chatting to told me she was a comptometer operator. I had no idea what a comptometer was, but it sounded terribly scientific and I made the right appreciative noises of someone who was impressed. In time I discovered that in essence it was the forerunner of the calculator and quite possibly she could have been a check-out girl. Anyway, she looked to me like at girl who was good with her hands. Pity we had to get off the train at Derby as they carried on to Loughborough. There were occasions when it was so wonderfully sunny that we never got past the Anglers Rest in Miller's Dale and spent the time drinking by the riverside until it was time to catch the train back to Derby! Life was good and it did not matter. The main thing was to enjoy ourselves.

A climb that we did tackle during sober moments was called the Virgins Crack which had a difficult move requiring you to stretch a leg and jam your boot in a crack then take a swing of faith hoping you would find the necessary handhold that lay out of sight around the corner in the crack. The problem was that if you failed to grasp the unseen handhold, then in all likelihood you could be in for a nasty accident if the foot you had previously jammed in the crack did not come free as you fell. The loud crack of snapping of bones would be swiftly followed by agonising screams and a leg with a bend in it that not been there before. It was not as if we were particularly afraid of falling off. We did it all the time.

I was always a far better caver than ever I was a climber and certainly as a caver I consumed more beer than was good for me. It seemed to come with the territory. After an exhaustive day underground, a hearty meal would be followed by some hearty drinking and this was certainly the order of the day during my weekend trips to the Mendips. In those far off times the Queen Victoria pub in Priddy (the wall sign used to have the brewer's name Courage above Queen Victoria, thus reading Courage Queen Victoria, which she would certainly need on a Saturday night!) was a mecca for cavers especially at weekends where it would be crammed to overflowing with rowdy, rugged cavers singing folk-type songs heavily laced with double-entendres, or more often than not just honest to goodness, down to earth, no nonsense sing-alongs of uncensored filth! The air inside the pub would be thick with cigarette smoke, beer fumes and more than a hint of sweaty neoprene from unwashed bodies. At the end of the evening the most that any of us had to do was stagger across the forecourt and up a flight of stone steps that lead to a communal bunkhouse where if you were lucky you might just grab a few hours of sleep. It almost goes without saying that there would be some pretty chronic snoring to contend with as well as belching, passing wind, scratching and the grunts and squeals of carnal copulating on a shaking bunk bed. Anyway, I remember one night in particular after everyone had finished whatever it was they were doing in their beds and had finally settled down being woken in the night by the rank odour of vomit. In the darkness I could see little as the room light had been switched off and stayed that way as we all knew our way in the darkness to the lavatory like homing pigeons, so I went back to sleep. Morning broke and the grey light of day penetrated the fogged-up windows and the haze and stench of rancid bodies, passed wind and the still lingering aroma of someone having been sick. As everyone got underway, it was quickly discovered that the culprit was a lad who had been so plastered that he had fallen asleep on his back and at some stage during the night had thrown up over his own face without even waking. It was not a pretty sight to look at just before breakfast. He lay completely motionless. Some girl who professed to have no medical knowledge beyond 'O' level Biology suggested he might be dead. Well if that was the case then one thing was certain, there was not going to be a queue of volunteers to give him the kiss of life, in fact no one wanted to go anywhere near him as he lay on his bed with his self-styled *'Phantom of the Opera'* face mask. After a while one of his mates prodded him with his foot and a faint gasp came through the crusted surface of the suspected corpse, so we left him in his squalor and went downstairs for breakfast. Now despite the fact that I had felt a tad unwell all night due to an overfill of Courage ale, I held out until I was about to cross the yard to the bar where breakfast was being served when my stomach seized-up and emptied itself in front of me and a couple of my mates. "'Feeling better?" one of them asked grinning from ear to ear. "You don't want to miss breakfast." And no I did not. Wiping the dribble from my face I joined the rest of the group in the bar, sat down and devoured an energy boosting breakfast of fried eggs, bacon, sausage, mushrooms, tomato, baked beans and fried bread, and never did breakfast taste so good! Then we all went back underground for the day. I think for the time being that is enough about drink as I am beginning to feel the need for a beer and I gave up drinking some years ago. When I look back on all the alcohol I must have drunk, all the money I must have spent, all the sickness and unforgiving hangovers in what at the time was deemed to be pleasure, I cannot help thinking that perhaps the Temperance Society really did have a point after all.

A Photo Finish

Going to work did allow me to have money in my pocket, but at the same time it was very interruptive to my social life, especially as I had to work a full week and every other Saturday morning which really loused up the weekend. But the occasional highlight came along, the best being the day I was told that a very large Victorian collection of stuffed birds and animals had been presented to the Museum Service by the Whitworth Institute at Darley Dale. Sadly they had been stored for many years in a damp cellar and needed to be sorted to salvage the best of the bunch, and I was given the task of dismantling all the cases which suited me down to the ground. The director left the job to me for she was well aware of my ardent interest in Taxidermy and knew that I had dabbled in the art in the past. Fortunately she did not ask me to show her anything I had done, for the memory of 'Quasimodo' the badly stuffed, hunch-back rabbit that ended its days in the dustbin still haunted me. Because of the vast amount of cases involved they were delivered and housed in a subsidiary building around the corner on Kedleston Road. The collection came with another of minerals and fossils, but they were to be sorted and identified by a geologist. Apart from going back to the main building for my tea breaks I would spend the entire day alone busily working my way through the cases which contained everything from foxes, badgers, hares, stoats, and hedgehogs to hundreds of birds from the humble House Sparrow to a Golden Eagle along with a case brimming with brightly coloured tropical Humming birds. Many had suffered beyond repair as their heads or legs came away in my hand as I tried to gently prise them from their dioramas. Often the mammals would be okay apart from being faded on their show sides, so Paul came up with the idea of restoring their colour using hair dyes (his friend was a hairdresser…say no more!) and to a degree it worked, although many were beyond anything that even Grecian 2000 professed to restore! One of the unexpected bonuses I discovered while tearing apart the background structures of plaster and paper was that the crumpled newspapers were obviously of considerable vintage and contained some very interesting advertisements. For example, I could have '365 shaves for only 6d with no blotches under my chin' if I used Vinolia Shaving Cream, and for that unruly facial hair I could 'train an untidy moustache into perfect subjection' with a bottle, only 3/6d (three shillings and sixpence old money) of Carter's Thrixolene. My baldness could be cured with 'Dr Weber's Comazone' at only 3/9d a bottle (I must order some of that immediately) and rid myself completely of gout with 'Reynold's Medicine', a mere 2/9d a bottle. Now that I was looking healthy and neatly hirsute I could finish off my dapper image with a pair of 'Super Contigo Shirts' at only 10s for two, plus a bargain pair of 'Ventilated Braces' (Why would you want to ventilate your braces?) for only 4s. The following I mention purely from curiosity and I want to make that perfectly clear from the outset that I have no intention of buying a 'Woman's Rust-Proof Corset' and 'English Stays' for only 4s, and a pair of, and heaven only knows why anyone would want these, 'Metallic Nipple Shields' for a shilling that apparently 'hold on like Limpets'. I guess if you lived by the seaside there was nothing stopping you from using the real thing and save yourself a shilling. I found it all fascinating along with reports of the Relief of Mafeking where the beastly Boers were giving old Baden-Powell a bit of trouble, but in the end our chaps won the day with the leader of the Boers, officer Elaf finally surrendering to 'BP' (as he was called) who promptly invited him to supper, so that was alright then! Inevitably, some of the stuffed specimens found their way into my bedroom back home which for a number of years had closely resembled a private museum. In fact the only thing that looked totally out of place was the bed.

There were times when it felt like all work and no play for one night of the week I took an evening class to re-sit my GCE 'O' level Biology examination which I had failed at school through paying more attention to the enticing biology mistress than the lesson she was giving, and another night studying for my 'A' level Art. This took place in the old purpose built Art College in Green Lane which is a magnificent example of Gothic/Arts and Craft style architecture and over one hundred and thirty years old. The night class tutor turned out to be my former art teacher from Joseph Wright School so that made the sessions more relaxed and enjoyable. Part of the syllabus involved life drawing which I had never done before and I suddenly found myself confronted one evening by a naked woman of a maternal disposition sitting on a chair in the centre of the room. We were told that it was all about shape, light and shade. Well she certainly had ample shape in the form of rolls of stomach, hanging breasts and a facial expression that seemed to imply she was sitting on something disagreeable. It could simply have been a touch of haemorrhoids, but I could not stop wondering just how good the biology mistress might have looked in her place. The end result was I passed both exams and moved onto something else.

That something else was another night class in Zoology which for some reason included botany. I did not realise this when I signed up for the course. I loathed botany. Any mention of the word botany was almost sufficient to put me to sleep quicker than any anaesthetist and after a long day at work that is precisely what would happen. My eye lids grew increasingly heavy as the lecturer droned on about stamens and anthers until my head hit the desk-top with a thud, whereupon I would instantly be awake facing the glare of the tutor, and to think I had paid hard earned cash for this. It is quite bizarre to think that in later life I became a reputable Royal Horticultural Society 'Gold Medallist' botanical artist, yet I still never bothered to learn the names of all those twiddly bits and pieces that make up a flower head. Anyway, the zoology part was far more interesting as week by week we had to dissect a frog. Sadly, week by week it was the same old frog. On week one he looked admirably 'froggish' until I cut him down the middle and pinned him spread-eagled out on a board where he seemed to lose some of his charm. Each week he was dragged out from heavens knows where and I had to proceed to remove a bit more of him and draw the bit in my text book along with a description of the its function. By week four 'froggy' was not looking too good and certainly not smelling too good either. He had gone very crispy around the edges and the remaining organs yet to be probed and prodded smelled fetid and well past their sell-by date. A young girl in the class who clearly had very sensitive nostrils and spent the entire lesson with a tissue stuck to her face boldly suggested to the tutor that perhaps we could all have a fresh frog to work on. The tutor looked at her aghast. He reacted in a similar manner as Mr Bumble the Beadle when *Oliver Twist* asked for more gruel. A fresh frog was totally out of the question. Considering the fees we had all paid and totting up the number of students in the class, I reckoned that the price of a fresh frog, ounce for ounce, must have been on a par with Beluga caviar! Shortly after this episode my interest waned and I left the course.

I decided to try my hand at obtaining a Naturalist Certificate as I had always fancied myself as a bit of a Charles Darwin as a glance around my bedroom would testify. This Certificate was a correspondence course requiring me to record and write every aspect and change taking place in two differing environments. This was no problem for within reach of a short cycle ride from home was a field with a pond close by Breadsall railway station and north of the village some dense woodland. All went splendidly for a month or two until I was informed that the course required me to attend a week of study at Flatford Mill over the other side of the world in Suffolk. This was too far to travel to by bicycle so I would have to put my hand in my pocket for a costly train ticket along with the cost of the course and accommodation. My bank balance told me to forget the idea. This famous mill featured in a painting by Constable. He of course, never had to pay a penny as his dad lived in the mill... alright for some! Undaunted, I persevered with another idea which was to ask the director of the Museum Service if she would back me in trying to study for the Museum Technicians certificate which she agreed to do, despite telling me that I was such a valued worker she would not want to lose me. I think she knew there would be no chance of that happening because the only way I could get on the course was to be working in a real museum, and all the applications for assistant jobs in real museums required you to already hold the Museum Technicians certificate. Whichever way I turned I was well and truly stuffed. The only option left open to me was suicide (yet again) which had its advantages for by now another expensive birthday 'fresh cream cake' fiasco loomed on the near horizon. Life was heavily stacked against me. Perhaps I should start going to church and ask to be forgiven for leaving Sunday school as a kid because they stopped giving out picture cards, and come clean about looking at Marlene Dexter's knickers as she sat opposite me in a field at the Whitsuntide Sunday School Treat near Coxbench in 1950. Actually I do not think she minded as she let me hold hands with her as later we were all made to dance around in a circle after the picnic. Mind you I must have looked irresistible to most of the girls in my white shirt with tie, grey socks and sandals and my trousers held tantalisingly just above the knee by a pair of braces. Pretty natty dressing for a five-year-old. Just as I was wondering which would be the least messy way of topping myself a light, in fact to be more exact, a photographic light shone at the end of my dark tunnel and proved to be my salvation. It turned out there was a disused dark-room tucked away at work and someone decided it would be beneficial for the cataloguing of exhibits if there was the occasional photograph taken for record purposes. I was given the job of cleaning out the old dark-room and getting it operational once more with me at the helm having convinced the director I knew something about photography. This claim was based purely on my amateur efforts on the home front, but once again and much to my relief nobody asked for any evidence. There had in the past been a bit of a photographic streak running in the family on my father's side which I hoped would fire my enthusiasm and guide me when necessary, for I was certainly going to need more than a little luck to pull this one off.

My father had always been an avid photographer and as a young man he had worked for the nationwide and well established firm of Jeromes which had premises in Derby next to Woolworths in Victoria Street. Here you could have your photograph taken, have your own photographs developed and printed and even buy a Jeromes roll of film for your next session. For a mere 2d (two old pennies) you could have your black and white photograph made into a postcard, or a sepia-toned version for only 5d. Quite what my father's role was nobody can recall, but in the staff photograph I have of him taken with a bevy of beauties he appears to have an expression of delight on his face. Centre stage is taken by a rather handsome woman looking a cut above the rest of the staff dressed in a black box-shoulder overcoat and sporting on her head a natty Schioparelli hat making her look as though she had just stepped out of a Bette Davis film. The following year shows my father in the staff photograph with even more beauties and looking like the cat that got the cream. The 1941 picture shows him centre stage dressed like Errol Flynn with a self-assured, devil-may-care look and surrounded by eight lovely ladies. The war was an obvious interruption for everyone, but he is back again in 1946 as the only man among eight glamour girls looking like a man with wicked thoughts on his mind, aimed at I would imagine, the young girl he is tucked into beside him. My father had been a good looking man despite his years of ill health for even as a child he suffered from attacks of asthma and had lived some of the time in Buxton where the air was purer. He lost a lung when young yet it deterred him from little in life. I use the word 'lost' with some reservation for it is a rather casual and somewhat misguided use of the word as it suggests a degree of carelessness over what is normally a serious event. People have always said things like, 'Oh yes, he lost an eye some years ago' or 'I remember now, he lost a leg when he was still quite young' implying reckless behaviour and irresponsibility on the part of the owner. Is it, I wonder, possible to wake one morning and discover while putting on a sock that you are a foot and an attendant leg missing because you have 'lost' it? 'I could have sworn it was there last night' you announce to yourself in a surprised manner as you frantically search through the bed sheets and under the bed among all that fluff to no avail. 'Well I'm blowed!' you exclaim, 'I must have lost my leg!' The point being that my father did not really lose his lung insomuch as he had not inadvertently left it on the back seat of the top deck of a bus on his way home, especially in his case for he had not actually lost it anywhere as he still had it inside him. The culprit lung just gave up the ghost one day and hung there like an old party balloon you find three weeks later down the back of your sofa. It refused to work ever again.

Getting back to the photography, some years later after my father had moved on from Jeromes he started a photographic business with an uncle under the trading name of Carter & Deane which was their surnames. No pushing the boundaries there then for a catchy trading name! My uncle built a wooden shed in his back garden in Upper Boundary Road which became the centre of all operations. From here they went to photograph their clients with a Purma-Special camera which did not make life simple as its different shutter speeds were dependant on which way round you held the camera... complex or what! The shed was where the films were developed and housed an enlarger for printing out the finished product. The shed also doubled as a kennel where my uncle locked his pet Alsatian dog when she was on heat. I am not too sure where that actually fits into all this, but I just felt compelled to mention it along with trying to get an image out of my mind concerning two men in a small wooden shed with a bitch on heat. My mother who was an artist having once painted for Crown Derby porcelain would painstakingly and skilfully colour-tint the black and white pictures, which in those days was a bit of a novelty before the advent of easily accessible colour photographs. It would require more than a degree of patience to hand colour a group shot of the Rowditch Football Club, a regular client.

I became bitten by the photography bug and because I was earning money I was able to purchase a Kodak 8mm cine camera complete with a turret lens comprising of a normal, wide-angle and telephoto lenses. This was pretty advanced stuff provided I overlooked the fact that it was clockwork and had to be continually wound-up and the reel of film only lasted a couple of minutes requiring it to be removed and turned over halfway through to use the other side. The film then had to be sent off for processing and having been split down the middle and joined it would come back twice its length making a continuous, but very short film. The first time I tried it out was by a railway bridge near Mansfield Road where I filmed steam locomotives chugging back and forth along the line. Shortly afterwards on the Sunday Rambler's train and leaning precariously out of a carriage window I filmed the approach to Milford tunnel. Everything looked further away through the viewfinder, so when a train steaming the other way unexpectedly shot out from the smoky entrance I became horribly close to being decapitated and only just pulled back in time. It might have posed a conundrum for some unfortunate track maintenance staff to have come across my head lying between the tracks with three lenses sticking out of my face. The following day the *Derby Evening Telegraph* might well have had the headlines 'Head of Alien with Three Eyes found near Milford Tunnel'. However, there was no stopping me now as greatness beckoned on the near horizon and I swiftly moved onto my all-time blockbuster depicting the demise of the Grimshaw family and their home Errwood Hall built among the wild moorlands of the Goyt Valley. In actual fact my great aunt Harriet who had been the mayoress of Buxton during the war remembered the Grimshaws arriving in Buxton by horse and carriage on shopping trips and taking refreshments in the Cavendish Coffee shop. However, when I was at Errwood Hall in my guise as Cecil B DeMille it was 1966 at a time when the construction of the second reservoir, the Errwood was underway and I made a clever little map that showed the slow flooding of the valley as the opener for my film. Much land was lost under water, but at least the residents of Stockport could enjoy a cup of tea and a bath. Al came along as 'sherpa' because we thought we should camp for a few days by the ruins of the old hall to get a feeling for the place and had nothing to do with the fact that we were just too idle to walk from Buxton every day. He brought along his Philips portable tape recorder to play some classical music in our tent of an evening when the site was plunged into pitch-black darkness and the only company we had was our nearest neighbours lying in the hilltop cemetery behind the ruins. Yes, it was a tad spooky. During the day we dashed around the site with tripod and camera filming everything I thought needed filming and recording on the spot comments, which would be used in a commentary. I think we secretly fancied ourselves as Fyfe Robertson, the bearded Scottish eccentric who was a roving reporter for the BBC programme *Tonight*. Some weeks later when the films had come back from processing and I had spent hours labouring over the editor getting giddy and feeling sick from the fumes of the film cement, my masterpiece was finally ready including a taped commentary voiced over the melodic sound of a Chopin piano piece and read by Al's cultured brother who had a sort of BBC voice making it all very professional if not a little posh. I was eventually ready to release the premier of my film (with a cast of thousands of rhododendron bushes) at the Cannes Film Festival, which in reality turned out to be the living room at home with a noisy, clanking projector, a Boots roll-down plastic screen hung from the ceiling and a Grundig tape recorder that failed to keep up with the film. Fortunately I had not invited any royalty, or famous personalities from the world of stage and screen, just the immediate family who had not managed to come up in time with a viable reason for being elsewhere. I felt as a movie director it was my finest hour, well twenty minutes as reels of film were expensive and I was working on a very small budget. The sad thing is that all my films of locomotives and the Goyt valley would now be classed as valuable archive material, but they all disappeared somewhere down the line during one of my many moves and is certainly a reason for me to say, 'If only I'd known!' and been more diligent.

Meanwhile, back in the dark-room at work I beavered away taking photographs and producing some grainy, grey and white photographs which should have been black and white, but only ever seemed to turn out grey and white. There was something going off here that I did not know about. I suggested to my boss Paul that I should visit a forthcoming Photographic Exhibition at Olympia to try and pick up some tips. The director generously paid for the train fare and said I should take the works camera with me and bring some pictures back of the advertised 'professional photographic studio opportunities' whatever they might be. When I arrived at Olympia the place was bustling with people milling around the hundreds of stalls all trying their hardest to sell their wares to anyone they could interest which included a miscellany of items that could only be classed as remotely connected to photography. Anyway, I mooched about for a while trying to look the business when above the general din an announcement was made saying that the first photo opportunity of the day was about to take place, so I joined the thronging mass and was swept away on a tidal wave of 'would-be' photographers towards a nearby stage. Determined to get a good view of whatever was about to happen I fought my way to the front of the crowd which had now become a mass of flailing arms, cameras and tripods and quickly realised their fervour, for a blaze of powerful spotlights were switched on to illuminate four scantily clad young women. They pranced around to Nancy Sinatra's *These Boots are made for Walking,* strutting their stuff and thrusting every part of their anatomy that was thrustable at the melee of salivating, boggle-eyed photographers and lecherous, leering Lotharios who continued to jostle and elbow each other for a better view. The girls were well underway by now and haughtily paraded around the stage in their high-heeled, knee-length boots, fish-net stockings and suspenders and a waist-hugging basque over the top of which burst barely-held bosoms of eye-watering proportions. I have to admit that the whole thing took me quite by surprise having originally anticipated some kind of demonstration on studio procedures. However, as I was on the front row and almost within 'cable release' distance from this eye-popping show of gyrating all-female sexuality I reached for my camera and began to capture the 'photographic opportunity' adding to the overwhelming noise of clicking, whirring, snapping and more clicking of a hundred camera shutters accompanied by sighing and gasping as the crowd mounted a crescendo of unleashed, frenzied enthusiasm. Eventually the girls with pouting lips threw farewell kisses to the crazed mob that were drooling and baying for more, raising the temperature even further as they all left the stage followed by an unseen, unfettered wave of testosterone that swept across the empty stage in hot pursuit. The crowd slowly dispersed and I made my way to one of the many eateries to console my feeling of anti-climax with a cup of tea and an iced bun topped with a cherry. I reflected on what a first class show of legs, thighs, buttocks, boobs and pouting faces it had been and I had recorded it with my camera, and unfortunately that was all I had recorded and all I had to show for my paid trip to Olympia. What was I going to show the director upon my return to work?

The following day at work everyone was enquiring as to whether I had had a good day. "Yes" I replied. "It was really interesting." Paul then asked "And did you take some good pictures?" Hesitating for a moment I replied that I thought there might be one or two good shots and I knew that very soon the director was going to ask to see them! 'Oh, b...' I thought to myself, there is no way I am going to get out of this. In fact I will be lucky if I get out alive! And so, as sure as 'eggs is eggs' the command came via the office that the director would like to see me and my photographs. The truth is the director was generally a fair-minded woman, but what I thought was cause for concern what that she was a woman and my photographs were all of… well… women, and in an advanced state of undress. In many ways I found her quite fearsome because she was very authoritative, so it was with more than a little trepidation that I stood outside her door one afternoon awaiting my fate. I took a sharp intake of breath and knocked on her door, and clutching my pictures in a very sweaty hand I entered the inner sanctum. After the initial pleasantries were over about my day out, I sheepishly handed over my photographs. With her spectacles perched on the end of her nose she scrutinised for some time each and every photograph showing no facial movement and making no sound. I fidgeted in my seat while trying to appear nonchalant and wondering how I could pay the train fare back when I would be penniless and out of a job. At last after what seemed an eternity she placed the pictures face-down in front of her, and leaning across the desk on both elbows she fixed me with her penetrating eyes and calmly said 'I don't think they've come out too badly. What do you feel?'

It was very obvious to me that the results coming out of the dark-room were really not that good and something was amiss in my technique. I still felt keen to pursue photography, but at the same time I obviously had a lot to learn. Late that summer I handed in my letter of resignation informing my colleagues that I had been accepted as a 'mature' student at the new college on Kedleston Road for a three year course in Creative Photography and would be enrolling in September. I was really looking forward to starting as a full-time student despite it being three years of study and three years of poverty. But all was not lost. Thankfully I would not have to suffer living in some unspeakable, shared, student doss house for I was about to become a married man.

If Only I'd Known!

Something for the Weekend, Sir?

One of the major requirements for marriage or at least it was in my day was a female which meant first having a girlfriend and my track record in that department was abysmal to say the least. I really had not tried very hard having been distracted by other things in life. It was not as though I had been totally devoid of encounters with the opposite sex, it was more a case of mishandling. For example, there had been Penny Walton when I was about fifteen who lived in one of those pre-fabricated houses near the racecourse that had been erected as post-war temporary accommodation but which in truth lasted for decades. Anyway, she quickly tired of going around with me because all I had to wear was my school jacket, which in today's parlance would be classed as 'lame', so I had to pester my mother to buy me a casual jacket. This she eventually did and brought home a 'pretend leather-look' black jacket that was in fact made out of PVC (poly-vinyl…er…concoction) which I have to admit I felt pretty top-notch in until some mate at school said it was just a rubber jacket. This knocked my image a little and Penny simply went off with another boy, thus amply demonstrating the fickleness of women and the unexpected non-pulling power of a PVC rubber jacket. Valiantly I wore it all through that hot summer refusing, despite my mother's pleas to take it off, and regardless of the fact that my blood temperature rose to near boiling point while my face took on the permanent hue of a cooked lobster. Come to think of it I believe records were made out of poly-vinyl. I wonder if my jacket which was really quite a cheap one was manufactured from old 'long-play' records? Then there had been Linsey of course, the greyhound girl who went off the boil after I had refused to come down stairs at home to see her because I was having a GCE examination revision strop. You can already see how my amorous involvements are looking decidedly pathetic and it only gets worse! There was the inefficient and far from successful grapple with a girl I met at a party held at Black Rocks who I inadvertently escorted over the edge of a drop in the dark. Amazingly this did not curb her desire and a week later she appeared outside my house in the back of a car driven by my friend Pete from Ripley which is where she also lived. On seeing me she leapt out of the car and pinned me up against my own privet hedge, demanding to know, rather aggressively why I had not been to see her and was I going to take her out or what? Now cycling to Ripley which I had done many times would not have been as far as cycling to see Maggie at Crich had I followed that through, plus the possible lure of rampant sex at the end of my journey held quite an appeal, yet I somehow managed to let the whole thing slip through my fingers and she stormed off in a huff. Not surprisingly, I never saw her again. The reality of the situation was that only a couple of days before her arrival I had bought myself a new tape recorder and did not have funds to spare to take her anywhere. At least you can switch a tape recorder off when you have had enough of it. I also befriended a girl when I was attending evening class for my 'A' level Art. Her line was that she was bored with her boyfriend so could she tell him she was going out with me and thereby be rid of him. This came out of the blue one evening as we were walking to the bus stop after class with her looping her arm in mine and adopting a fawning manner by pressing her body against me. That was fine by me, but at this stage of the game the words 'being used' sprung to mind and as there had been no mention of a reward for being the bait and for all I know her boyfriend could have been some violent thug who at the slightest provocation would happily alter the shape of my head. I declined the invitation. I hope you appreciate just how prudent it was of me not to pursue this one.

The thing is, my close friends all had girlfriends and were thinking of getting hitched or had already tied the knot. At this stage I was acutely aware that very shortly I could become the proverbial 'Billy-no-mates' and left to wander the world alone. As I was now twenty years old and without any form of female attachment, I might get called a social leper or be recommended for medical treatment, such was the peer pressure back then. It was not just girls who would feel themselves left on the shelf if they had not got betrothed by their early twenties. However, just as things were looking bleak, that is, bleaker than usual my friend Pete invited me to a party at Ripley. It was a warm summer evening so I turned up looking cool in shirt sleeves, and yes I was wearing trousers as well and I mingled among the thronging crowd of virtual strangers. I have never been one for parties and was considering this to be a serious mistake. Pete was busy with his girlfriend in fact most of the lads were busy with their girlfriends (for busy read, passionate clinches, frenzied snogging and devouring each others face with an occasional break for air) and dancing to a background rhythm of the Beach boys belting out *I Wish They all Could be Californian Girls*. At that precise moment in time I would certainly have settled for a Californian girl, or one from Mablethorpe, Timbuktu, or even Outer Mongolia! Then I spied her standing alone by a window.

She appeared to be having about as much fun as I was which was very little. The only thing going for me was the free beer. She was gentle-looking, trim, fair-haired with pale skin and seemingly unattached. I approached and said something to her along the lines that she looked as though she knew as many people at the party as I did, which was almost none. This turned out to be the case and we fell into conversation whereupon she told me she lived at nearby Heanor and worked in a solicitor's office as a Conveyancing Clerk in St Mary's Gate in Derby. Things went quite well for the remainder of the evening and we agreed to meet the following weekend. The next Saturday saw me well turned out in a clean shirt, trousers and my hair plastered down with Brilliantine (did you know that the film *Grease* in French was... you're right , I've done that bit already) which was the poor man's Brylcream. It came in an oval tin with one of those lids that snaps your fingernail off 'Gestapo' fashion while you struggle to remove the top. It was green in colour, slightly whiffy and the consistency of axle grease and could have unfortunate side effects. A friend of mine told me when he wore it as a lad that unbeknown to him it attracted flies as though he was wearing a cow pat on his head, and of course once they landed on the grease they were stuck fast as if on fly paper. This caused passing folk to stare at his unusual hair style, wondering no doubt as to why he had dotted his hair with what seemed to be raisins along with a cloud of flies buzzing above his head. I even had a shave that evening splashing on some Old Spice aftershave (Ye Gods! that stings!) before leaping onto the saddle of my trusty steed to cycle the long road from Chaddesden to Heanor. I pedalled furiously up hill and down dale along the sparsely populated A608 like a man in the Tour de France chasing the coveted 'yellow shirt'. I whizzed past the Three Horseshoes (I could do with a pint) near Morley, then away down the road past the Rose & Crown (Phew, I could murder a pint now) at Smalley Cross, and beginning to noticeably flag I groaned past The Bell (Drink! Drink! My tongue has just got caught in the spokes of the front wheel) at Smalley before slogging up the hill to Heanor. Carol, for that was her name lived in a small neat detached house fronted by a tiny lawned garden. I knocked on the front door hopefully not looking too hot and sweaty. Carol greeted me with a smile and led me into a back room where her parents were seated at a table. I hoped I was not going to be subjected to some kind of interrogation. I was immediately taken aback to see that her parents were quite an elderly couple and it struck me at the time that Carol, their only child had plainly just got out in time with her mother's menopause hot on her heels! We all engaged in the normal preliminary chit-chat, had a nice cup of tea and as it was a fine warm summer evening (Remember those? No I didn't think so.) Carol suggested the two of us should go for a walk and take along their ageing dog Randy. We strolled down a lane that skirted the edge of an old colliery and with the birds singing in the hawthorn hedge, the warmth of the sun on our faces and the heaps of rusting scrap iron visible through a sagging chain link fence, we held hands for the first time. Romance was definitely in the air. There was also a crazed dog in the air that appeared from nowhere and flew at great speed towards old Randy. If Randy, and I hate to think how he came by that name, did once hang onto the back of peoples legs simulating a furious act of fornication then thank goodness he was now past all that. Nevertheless, he still quickly, well as quickly as an old arthritic dog is able, took on a defiant stance with a display of snarling, his lips curled back showing the intimidating gaps of missing teeth. Within seconds all hell was let loose and the air became filled with a cacophony of yapping, growling, barking, yelping and screaming, the latter from Carol who feared she may find herself dragging home a dead Randy on the end of his leash. This would have been a fair synopsis of the situation given the fact that the mad attacker was on top of old Randy baring his full set of teeth and poised ready to tear out some serious bits of dog, or to be more precise some serious bits of Randy. During this noisy fracas it dawned on me that the onus had fallen to me to break up the fight by some means or other as soon as possible. Now from where I was standing it did not look very likely that either dog was willing to sit down and talk this situation through sensibly, so I grabbed the assailant by the scruff of its neck, booted it up its rear end and sent it on its way. By the time we had got back to the house the story of my heroic deed had grown out of all proportion and it had become a modern day version of St George slaying the dragon, or in this instance a mangy mongrel with a piece missing from one ear. After Carol had related the tale to her parents she was all but ready to swoon with admiration at the very thought of my fearless intervention. I finally got a kiss off her, but only after she had cuddled and kissed old Randy first, who was busily wolfing down a late dinner. Was it my imagination or was there really a lingering hint of 'PAL' in that first kiss? According to the dog food manufacturers, 'PAL prolongs active life'. I wonder if it works for humans? Either way, that first kiss was meaty in more ways than one.

We started dating on a regular basis and it all began to look like the real thing. Sometimes we would go for a walk with 'four legs' in tow, or catch a bus to Nottingham and go to the cinema and see a film. The very first film we saw was *Catch Us If You Can* which was really a showcase for the pop group the Dave Clark Five and not very good. I can only remember bits of it. I think there were some lads and a girl racing about on a beach in a Mini-Moke, then a lad and a girl frolicking about in some snow, and that was that. It was obviously not a memorable film despite being directed by the great John Boorman. He was responsible for many great films and was an accomplished director. Who can forget the truly toe-tapping banjo duelling in *Deliverance* that would make a man with only one leg get up and hop about? A favourite of mine to this day is *Hope and Glory* depicting so brilliantly the time and circumstances of war on the home-front all laced with 'down to earth' comedy. Another film we saw together was *The Knack* starring a sultry dark-eyed, dark-haired, cap-wearing Rita Tushingham, the smoothy Ray Brooks and lots of girls in white, tight-fitting, pointy-breasted sweaters. Ah, halcyon days! I seem to have got carried away and had better get back to the matter in hand namely the growing relationship with my fair maid. It was often a little late by the time we arrived back at Carol's home, which because her parents normally went to bed quite early gave us the opportunity for a canoodle on the sofa, at least that was the idea. The problem was that we were continually being interrupted by her mother.

"Carol! Carol! What are you up to? It's gone ten-thirty you know."

"Yes mother I know."

Then perhaps ten minutes later there would be another shout from upstairs.

"Carol! Carol! You're still not upstairs. Isn't it time you said goodnight?"

"Okay mother, I won't be long"... and so it went on, and on, and on until we got the final warning.

"Carol! Carol! You should have been in bed some time ago. It's very late. You must be up to no good at this hour. I'd better come down and see what's going off."

Yes we were getting up to no good, or would be if only you would shut up and stop bellowing down the stairs every five minutes and continually interrupting our attempts to get up to no good! Getting up to no good proved to be very hard work indeed and our passions went up and down like a yo-yo after which I would then have to cycle home. This was starting to put years on me. Eventually I was allowed to stay overnight in the strictly forbidden, no hanky-panky front bedroom. I was convinced her mother had put electronic sensors under the carpet. I was definitely confined to quarters.

During these stays I got to know Carol's parents as much as I could which was not as simple as it sounds particularly if I happened to get into conversation with her father whose ill-fitting false teeth and broad 'Tag Hill' dialect made for a deadly and challenging combination. Tag Hill is I understand an area that falls around the first long incline into the suburbs of Heanor itself, which for reasons unknown had developed its own brand of Debyshire dialect. I recall one icy morning after I had stayed the night getting my bike ready for the ride back home when her father sidled up to me and said, "Wattas froz ta'dee, 'appen thee'll bi coder wiv th'arse froz ta seeat." For much of the time his speech was unintelligible unless you happened to be a passing visitor from planet Zob, in which case could you please explain it to me! Another time we somehow got onto the subject of sex which completely threw me off my guard.

"Doosta yoos wiv'drool meethod lad?" he enquired with a gappy grin.

"Er... what?" I stammered

"Tha nors, wivdrool. Tha taks thee ol' todger owta last minit like" he repeated peering at me and waiting for an answer. I looked back at him biting my lip. I could not for the life of me think of anything to say. The truth is I really wanted to be somewhere else. Even a condemned cell or the French guillotine would have been acceptable.

"Allus wok'd fir me" he enthused. "Fulpruf thet is lad, fulpruf."

It did not seem to have occurred to him as it had to me that the very fact I was dating his daughter strongly suggested that his withdrawal method was far from fool-proof, but I felt disinclined to point this out to him and possibly cause an argument as I was really quite uncomfortable with this conversation and where it might be going. Luckily, old Randy who had been lying close by suddenly leapt into life from his former moribund state and began noisily snuffling and ravaging his genitalia with such fervour that I suggested he might have a flea, thus steering the conversation onto a less personal topic. "Tha cudst bi reet" he replied, poking about between the dogs legs. "Best git DDT poowda' an' gee'im a doustin." I recall my granny having a next door neighbour who had ill-fitting teeth, or possibly none at all, and she had problems with her diction. For example, if you should be daft enough to engage her in conversation and ask her what she was having for tea, then the answer could well be 'tum toddin toshigers'. I will let you work it out for yourselves.

Occasionally I would stay over for the entire weekend and disappear for hours in the rear garden. The garden was huge with an old orchard, but the object of my disappearing act was a very extensive shed in which I spent many pleasant hours for inside it was an Aladdin's cave of objects from the past most of which had belonged to Carol's grandfather, a Yorkshire man who had long departed this earth. He had been a master carpenter or cabinet maker in his time and had produced all manner of furniture over the years. He even steamed the wood to produce the curves necessary for chair backs and arms. Beneath the layers of dust and cobwebs lay a stack of hardwood including oak, apple wood and the much sought after Cuban Mahogany. Stored in boxes was an array of tools, many of which defied description and used for goodness knows what, but which in skilled and knowledgeable hands had created fine pieces of work. Dozens of wooden moulding planes lay on a bench that carved out incredible complex edging along the side of a board and each tool had his name engraved on it. I was given a free hand to use anything I thought would be useful and spent hours happily rummaging among one man's possessions from the past. I might have passed my 'O' level Woodwork, but I was not capable of attaining his expertise for here was a man who could probably chisel out a secret mitred dovetail joint with his eyes closed. I am afraid that a tenon joint was to be my best shot!

And so life trundled ever onwards with me still cycling to Carol's house on a regular basis and occasionally meeting her in Derby during the lunch hour as her place of work was not too far from where I worked. I eventually suggested that she might like to spend a weekend at my house, especially as my parents were far more lenient and would not be shouting theirselves hoarse every five minutes asking what we were up to or even thinking of getting up to. This would save me the long ride which was sometimes quite taxing if I had had a trying day. There was one winter evening in particular when I left work, got to Chester Green only to find it completely underwater as recent rain had caused the Derwent to burst its banks and come flooding at a great rate of knots down Mansfield Road like the Amazon in full spate. I soon gave up the idea of trying to ride my bike through the water as it was far too deep, very cold and very threatening. It was strangely eerie for there was no traffic to be seen, just the sound of angry rushing water. Mansfield Road was the main waterway and I had trouble keeping upright as I tentatively crossed the road. There were a couple of hairy moments as hurtling down the flood came tree branches, boxes, planks of wood, in fact all manner of flotsam and jetsam that suddenly loomed out of the darkness bearing down on me at great speed and with murderous intent. I successfully dodged the onslaught and made it to higher ground and home. After drying out followed by a quick dinner ('you'll get indigestion bolting your food like that'…how right my mother was!) I was once again pedalling my way in the dark and through many deep puddles on the familiar slog to Heanor and growing older with every passing mile.

The weekend of Carol's stay approached and it had been arranged that I would let her have my bed and I would sleep on the sofa downstairs. This, I hasten to add was not my arrangement but I was not going to push my luck at this stage. It was of course, to deter any shenanigans I might have in mind. I mean, what sort of a person did they think their son was? Nothing could have been further from my thoughts! That really is a massive lie and now I will not be going to heaven. But it did not finish there, for as if to kill off any intent on my part my mother one evening prior to Carol's arrival, unexpectedly managed to bring what until then had been a normal conversation around to farmyard animals. Now according to the parables of my mother any form of sexual activity taking place within the confines of a farmyard will instantly arouse all the animals into a deafening crescendo of mooing, bleating, quacking, crowing, snorting, snuffling and sighing (sorry! that last one was the farmer's wife) and so on, and so on, because they can smell 'it'. Quite what 'it' was they could all smell she failed to explain and I was too taken aback to ask. Whether or not this was based on personal experience she also failed to explain. Somehow I think not as any hay dust would have sent my father off into one of his uncontrollable asthmatic coughing fits, thereby rendering him unfit to arouse the farm animals or even himself. This impromptu tale left me in a bit of a quandary as to whether or not it was true. Naturally the whole idea of having Carol over was for me to sneak upstairs when everyone was asleep and do the dastardly deed which had not been possible because of Carol's paranoid mother forever shouting downstairs with her time checks every five minutes. She could have got a job as the 'speaking clock'. But what I now had to consider was would I be found out when our two cats got wind of my doings by roaring upstairs to join each other in a chorus of unprecedented caterwauling while removing the paint from my bedroom door in a frenzy of clawing, thereby waking the entire household and the neighbour's howling dog who would be hell-bent on coming through the wall to join in the party. I began to feel unsure about this impending stay and wondered if my mother was just warning me off after failing perhaps to succeed with my sister's suspected skulduggery which will be related at a later date.

Friday night arrived and Carol and I came home from work together on the bus and so the scene was set. After everyone had retired for the night I lay wide awake on the sofa musing as to whether or not I should chance my arm. Predictably a young man must do what a young man must do, so I risked all and stealthily crept up the stairs, which until then had never creaked once in their entire life, and joined Carol in my bed. All appeared to be going quite well, everything taking a normal course of events until we realised that unlike any self-respecting, well trained boy-scout I had not come prepared. I knew there and then that I should have joined the scouts all those years ago for then I would have 'dib-dibbed my dob' and 'ging-ganged my goolies' around a campfire and not be in the situation I was now facing. The hitherto unbridled passion sank like a lead balloon rather taking the edge off everything. Things went from bad to worse after a ten minute unsuccessful fiddle about with a polythene bag we called it a night and I sloped off downstairs in the worse state imaginable. The upshot of this totally useless, non-productive encounter was that both cats had slept through it all, thus making me question even more my mother's farmyard tale. Perhaps at this juncture I should tell you that nearly fifty years on I have been told by a very reliable and trustworthy source that my mother's story is in fact true, so you have been warned! I must ask my wife how she knows about this. Oh dear! I think I have just let the cat out of the bag! Guess who will be cooking his own dinner tonight?

Next morning everything seemed quite normal on the surface and presumably my nocturnal dalliance had gone unnoticed. Carol however, made sure it took centre stage the minute we were alone. "You've got to get a proper thing" she started in a serious tone. Up to this moment in time I had not had any experience of condoms. I recall as an inquisitive boy seeing what turned out to be one in the bottom drawer of my parent's bedroom. It was a heavy duty re-usable one lying like a pampered pet on a bed of cotton wool and coated with talcum powder. It resembled a short section of beige coloured bicycle inner-tube and its use puzzled me for years.

"A proper thing?" I repeated like a parrot.

"Yes, you know" she insisted, "some condoms."

"Oh right, some Durex."

"Precisely, some Durex."

"But I'll have to go to a chemist" I protested, "and it's always women behind the counter. I can't do that, it's too embarrassing".

"Oh for goodness sake you don't think I'm going to ask for them do you? They'll think I'm on the game." She had a point. "Can't you get some from a barber's shop?" she continued.

"It'll be full of blokes. I can't just go in and ask for some." By now I was becoming quite pathetic.

"Well go for a haircut then."

"I had a haircut last week. If I go again I'll be as good as bald" I complained.

"Well you'll just have to go again" she replied quite resolutely. "That business last night was just silly."

Clearly she was in no mood to give any quarter. The thing is that another haircut with my already receding hair would in all likelihood render me almost bald. I had heard that too much sex can make you bald, but I had not even started! That afternoon I sloped off to the barber shop at the top of the hill, all the time wishing I was sitting in the sunshine outside the Anglers Arms in Miller's Dale having a pint. I opened the door of the barbers quickly realising it was Saturday afternoon. It was heaving with mouthy youths and blokes arguing about football and 'what a pillock that goalie was last week who was too useless to even catch a cold'. I sat down and waited my turn. Eventually, with the shop continuing to fill with hirsute clients my turn came to sit in the swivel chair.

"How are we to day sir? Just a trim is it?" asked the all too jovial barber.

"Er, yes just a bit off" I replied, my mind focussed on the array of condoms spread out before me beneath the wall mirror. How would I know which packet to buy? I ran my eyes over the display of goods, some professing to be this, that and the other, and others which were normal, sensitive, super-sensitive and sky-blue-pink with knobs on. Luckily the barber left the room for a minute and went into the back of the shop, whereupon I seized the opportunity to grab a packet and rapidly conceal it in my clammy hand. He returned and finished clipping and snipping what bit of hair was left on my head to clip and snip, showed me the results in the 'mirror behind the back of the head' scenario and I got up to pay.

"Thank you very much sir, that'll be..."

"And these as well" I mumbled beneath my breath.

"I'm sorry, what did you... Ah, right, something for the weekend as well" he announced so everyone could hear. He then made matters worse by playing on my obvious embarrassment.

"Has sir tried the feather-light?" he grinned.

Sir of course had not tried the feather-light, in fact sir just wanted to leave the shop as quickly as possible. I handed over the money and with a face glowing like a Belisha beacon, convinced that the entire audience in the shop was sniggering and tittering at me, I rushed out into the fresh air. By now I could not stop myself from thinking what a lot of trouble all this sex business had caused me. 'Christ' I mumbled to myself, 'If only I'd known'. I knew I should have become a celibate monk and lived an uncomplicated existence. Women do have an awful lot to answer to! I also knew I could never go back to that hairdresser ever again.

That night armed with my purchases I once again mounted the stairs safe in the knowledge that the two cats would not be removing the paint from my bedroom door and the neighbour's dog would not be manically tunnelling through the wall and emerge salivating with a crazed look in his eyes. Only welcome peace would reign throughout the sleeping household and true love could run its uninterrupted intended course. WRONG!! Just as everything was going swimmingly and I was teetering on the threshold of no return, my father suddenly flung open his bedroom door, then paused outside our door having one of his coughing fits. Convinced that any second now he would be flinging open our bedroom door, I froze. However, he plodded downstairs to the lavatory and we waited, and waited. After what seemed like most of the night he was heard to emerge and then go into the kitchen. If he entered the living room then I would be scuppered for only an empty sofa would greet him. While all this was going on my ardour was cooling quicker than a freshly boiled egg in cold water. He finally came back upstairs and returned to his bed much to our relief. In the fullness of time the deed was done and I was able to creep back downstairs to my sofa. It had been an awful lot of anxiety, but as I lay there wide awake I could not help thinking to myself that in actual fact the whole escapade had not been half bad and I would definitely be giving it another go!

As things hotted up so to speak, we decided to get married like everybody else and we arranged to have the banns registered at St Lawrence's church in Heanor despite neither of us ever having stepped inside the place. Curiously, history records that St Lawrence was a bit of a fanatic who took it far too personal to my way of thinking when he discovered that the Romans were killing off all the bishops and deacons and his name was not on the list. Obviously feeling snubbed at being given the cold shoulder St Lawrence purposefully set about getting on the wrong side of a Roman prefect (was he barking or what?) who thought he was having a bit of a laugh at his expense and duly arrested him. The prefect determined to wipe the smile off St Lawrence's face hit on the idea of barbequing him to teach him a lesson. Well just how wrong could he be! Fiesty St Lawrence was chained in the nip to a large gridiron and suspended over some warming, glowing coals where apparently after a while he turned to the prefect and addressed him with a cheery smile requesting that he should be turned over so his other side could cook after which they could eat him. This outrageous display of flippancy understandably got right up the prefect's nose to such an extent that he went into a major strop, stormed off in a foul mood and in all likelihood took it out on the wife and kids back home. What history does not record is whether or not the assembled crowd took St Lawrence at his word by forming an orderly queue while some entrepreneurial soul walked down the line handing out bread baps. I cannot help but think that old St Larry was a bit of a wag!

Meanwhile, Carol and I had been summoned one evening to go to the church to meet the vicar who wished to take us through a practise session of the marriage ritual, so on the day we would say the right thing at the right time. That went off pretty smoothly and then the vicar insisted on demonstrating how we should walk back down the aisle together in a sedate manner. As I had been walking all my life I objected to this and wondered if he thought I might indulge in a showy display of a couple off cartwheels, half a dozen back-flips with a half-twist landing perfectly on both feet with my arms fully outstretched which might just take him of his guard. When we had finished all this nonsense and performed to his satisfaction and allowed to remove our 'L' plates, he then launched into a lecture on morals and something about saving our bodies until the sacred state of matrimony had been bestowed upon us. The thing is he was a bit late coming in with this one, as since the initial hiccup in my bedroom at home we had been at it like a warren full of rabbits at every opportunity that presented itself, and there had been many opportunities.

Looking to our married future we had managed to secure a small end terraced house on the south side of Derby which prior to moving in provided us with somewhere to escape at weekends on the pretext of doing a bit of decorating. Needless to say, decorating was way down the list of priorities. Purchasing the house had been within our means because Carol was able to do all the legal paperwork herself. Consequently we paid very little in legal fees and that was a great saving. The house cost us the princely sum of one thousand, nine hundred and ninety-five pounds and was situated a stone's throw from Rolls-Royce. I mention this in particular because somewhere close by there was presumably a forge of some kind with a drop-hammer that often vibrated through the house well into the night. Sometimes I would come downstairs in the morning thinking I had spent the night in the wrong house as all the furniture had been re-arranged by the reverberations of the drop-hammer. Okay, so that is a bit of an exaggeration, but it was a tiresome thump that often went on for hours.

Prior to the wedding there seemed to be endless excuses to meet friends of an evening and have protracted drinking sessions which normally took place in Derby as I now spent a lot of my time staying at Carol's house and so travelled into work with her on the bus from Heanor where I met a few of her friends. I recall a particular girl whose name escapes me (which she will be pleased about) whose claim to fame was being able to piddle into the top of a milk bottle without making any mess. I had to take her word for it as she never actually demonstrated this talent on a moving bus, and I presumed she now worked in a solicitor's office because her peculiar skill had been shelved as a career option. Her husband with her in tow, used to drive about in a Heinkel Messerschmitt which was a three-wheeled car with little emphasis on the word car, for with its plastic canopy it looked very much like the cockpit of a World War Two fighter plane, but one that had been mysteriously parted from its wings. She always sat behind her husband straddling the fuselage like pilot and navigator as they roared along the road with an engine that sounded like an ailing Messerschmitt. It was not a class vehicle. I only ever went out in the contraption once when her husband thought we should have a night out together which finished with a strip show in a working men's club near Codnor. The entertainment began with a comedian with a repertoire of jokes and vocabulary fresh from the sewer of life after which the stripper, who was not a good looker, sidled onto the stage, threw off her clothes, strutted her stuff then insisted on sitting on my knee and poking a breast into my face. Panache did not come into it and she continued to grin throughout with nicotine brown teeth most of which were in serious need of emergency dental treatment. Naturally it took time, but I did eventually recover from the experience.

Happily evenings out were not normally of this calibre and were enjoyable social events with friends. More often than not I had to finish my last drink in a hurry so Carol and I could say our farewells before rushing off to the bus station and by the skin of our teeth catch the last bus to Heanor. This could have serious drawbacks because it was a slow journey and I would have several pints of beer sloshing about inside me like an overfilled water bed and needed to be released as was the case on one such journey. There were barely a handful of revellers on board and we sat on the back seat away from everyone else. After about ten minutes the urge to piddle came on and increased with alarming rapidity until I was crippled with agony. It felt like both kidneys were being forced out over my trouser belt and the pain intensified as each minute ticked by. I just had to go. I initially thought of piddling on the bus safe in the knowledge that no one would know as we were at the very back, until I realised this plan would fail miserably when the bus started down a hill and everybody at the front would wonder why they were wearing wet shoes. I was now doubled up in pain and knew I just had to get off the bus. Carol bravely went to the front with me crawling behind and asked the driver if he would mind stopping the bus for a while as I was feeling very unwell.

"He'll only be a few seconds" she said in a cooing voice to the driver who clearly hated the late shift and just wanted to get home and have a beer in front of the telly.

"Not allowed to stop" he barked back. "Only at scheduled bus stops."

What a miserable old b....r I thought to myself clutching my bladder to me like a bag full of shopping.

"But I think he might be sick any moment" she continued with a smile still hoping to win him over.

At the mention of the word sick he slammed on the brakes, opened the door and I disappeared into the night quicker than you could spell out Mississippi. I managed to stagger around to the rear of the bus and simply let fly. It felt like Niagara Falls flowing out of my trousers and just as unstoppable. I was not long before the impatient driver was shouting something about getting out and seeing where I had gone and I could hear Carol trying to placate him. He was plainly annoyed at the length of time I had gone missing and began revving the engine furiously, whereupon I was consumed in a dense cloud of diesel exhaust fumes. I fought for breath fearing at any moment I might die of monoxide poisoning and be found lying lifeless in the road awash with my own urine. I quickly needed to move, so still piddling profusely I galloped out from behind the bus, across a pavement and into the hedge of a front garden. I could see passengers clearing the condensation off the bus window and peering out to see if they could spot me, and still I kept up a steady flow which by now in the cold night air had become a steaming stream across the pavement for all to see. I have no recollection of how long this mortifying dilemma lasted, but I did after a considerable length of time finally climb back on board the bus several years older from the strain and collapse back in my seat. The driver tried to wear an expression denoting both anger and intolerance, but came out as somewhat strained and pinched as if he was desperate to stifle a severe outburst of flatulence. I strongly suspect I had left my kidneys in the hedge bottom as my lower sides ached with pain. Ten minutes later we arrived at our stop and I fell out of the bus as my bladder had already re-filled and I was desperate to go again. I waited for the bus to grind away down the hill before propping myself up against a wooden fence to once more let loose the dogs of war. We walked along the dark alleyway together that lead to the street where Carol lived and I arrived at her house feeling like a rung out dishcloth. Thank heavens her mother was fast asleep, and thank heavens I was young, but I reckoned too much of this sort of trauma would soon take its toll. As for Carol, well I do not think she was best pleased with my performance and probably hoped that we would never have to face that particular bus driver ever again.

I remember the bus stop being on the crown of a hill by a shop that seemed to sell all manner of odds and ends. Here the alleyway started which we would walk down to get to Carol's home. I recently visited the area but had trouble locating the alley as it turned out the shop had been pulled down and replaced with a house set back from the road. I asked a local man who fortunately did not speak 'Tag Hill' where I had gone wrong and he soon put me on the right track. I strolled down memory lane, except memory lane had become a tip for rubbish and a public lavatory for every dog in the neighbourhood and the only sign of life I met was in the shape of an extremely mangy, scruffy cat that crept along like a mechanised, worn-out doormat. Carol's house still remains and looked prim and cared for even though the front garden was now a parking lot. Back along the main road I came across a pub with boarded over windows, chipped paint and an air of dereliction and abandonment.

It was called The Memory Lane, but had clearly lost its memory. In a way it said it all and I drove away a little dejected. In this instance there was some truth in the saying that you should never go back to visit old haunts.

Jumbo a Canine Misfit

Everything seemed to happen in 1966. Despite me being a few days under age and requiring parental consent to get married, my mother quietly held back her reservations about the whole thing knowing I would not take any notice anyway, so the wedding went ahead at the very end of April. In September of the same year I signed on at college for a three year course in Creative Photography whatever that meant. The wedding took place on a Saturday afternoon as was usual in those days. Carol wore a white flouncy dress and I decked myself out in a brown suit. I had been to John Collier the gentlemen's outfitters in Derby. There was a television jingle at the time which went, 'John Collier, John Collier, the window to watch' so I went along and watched the window of John Collier and quickly found myself the other side of the window watching my wallet rapidly empty as I ordered my wedding suit. However, on the day the sun shone, St Lawrence rung his bells and there were flowers everywhere, confetti everywhere along with hordes of people the majority of which I had never met. Likewise at the reception held in The White Horse by the square in Ripley. Masses of people thronged the room that for all I knew could have just come in off the street not wishing to miss the opportunity a free bite to eat while doing their shopping. After the rumpus and commotion had died down we were later given a quieter send off at Derby Midland station as the two of us waved goodbye from a train bound for Glasgow and a honeymoon by Loch Lomond. In truth the word 'honeymoon' for some inexplicable reason gives me the 'heebie-jeebies' and interestingly enough the dictionary describes it as, 'a period of unusual harmony (take note of the word unusual here) following the establishment of a new relationship, while the corpulent Dr Samuel Johnson defines it as, 'the first month after marriage, when there is nothing but tenderness and pleasure'. He of course was unmarried so I am not sure what his summation is based upon. The nearest encounter with a woman he probably had was being misunderstood by a reeking old hag in a squalid hovel in the highlands who took his request to examine her sleeping quarters (mere social curiosity) as a proposition to sleep with her, which flustered and disconcerted the man putting him into an 'unbearable state'. The point is that both definitions appear to strongly imply that wedded bliss will last no longer than a month after which it all begins to slide downhill. Only then can the couple get down to the realities of living with each other which probably means highlighting one another's short-comings, slagging each other off, arguing, shouting, throwing crockery (Oops! there goes Aunt Dorothy's Hornsea pottery coffee-pot wedding present) slamming doors and generally being moody and disagreeable toward each other, or to put it another way, fairly normal married rapture!

Back on the train we travelled overnight in a corridor coach arriving in Glasgow at some ungodly hour of the morning feeling weary, bog-eyed and generally dishevelled in all aspects. As first nights go it was not up to much, what with people coming and going all night long, slamming doors and talking noisily, little sleep was to be had and any idea of indulging in unbridled passion and sex even on the overhead luggage rack was completely out of the question. We hauled our cases to the bus station and caught a bus to Balmaha where we were collected in a van by Malcolm who I had known from childhood holidays. He drove us up the road chattering in some unintelligible dialect and doing a lot of grinning and elbowing until we arrived at Critreoch house where we were to stay for the week. The house overlooked Loch Lomond with wonderful views across the water to Luss on the far side, or that was the impression we got from the occasional glimpses between the showers of rain, drizzle and cloying mist. The first notable thing that happened was when Carol discovered she had lost her purse, and this is not a 'double entendre' she really did lose her purse. Because we lacked any transport of our own we were obliged to walk everywhere as the bus service appeared to be a local 'best kept secret' or a myth. This was a bit of a shame as walking in the rain for any length of time soon loses its novelty. Consequently, the second notable thing that happened was we went home. End of honeymoon! On reflection it could have been worse for our stay was pre-midge season so we avoided the added torment of being constantly enveloped in clouds of biting insects while being actively engaged in slapping at all parts of our bodies like demented dervishes doing the Highland Midge Dance.

Back in Derby we set about settling into home life and getting on with the overdue decorating. First up was wall-papering the living room in red flock (all the rage in the sixties) and covering the floor with mahogany parquet tiles (also all the rage in the sixties) which had to be stuck down, thus requiring me to spend hours on my hands and knees breathing in the heady, life-threatening fumes of a contact adhesive. The smell became so bad it invaded the entire house to such an extent that the only thought going through my mind apart from the obvious sense of panic preceding a lung transplant was to up sticks and live somewhere else. The last sizeable job was to make a cover out of wood-grain effect Formica (Yes, of course this was all the rage in the sixties, it goes without saying!) to hide a hideous Ascot gas water heater that hung menacingly over the end of the bath. It resembled something that might have been jettisoned near Cape Canaveral for every time it fired up there was a roar of flames at its base followed by a period of unsettling vibrations, giving the distinct impression that it was about to part-company with the wall and head off on a lunar mission. It was the most unnerving thing I have ever encountered in a bathroom, aside that is from periodic glimpses of my own image unclothed in a mirror.

As we were both working and did not spend a lot of our time at home it remains a mystery to me why Carol should take it upon herself to introduce a Guinea pig into the household. It was forever escaping during the day when we were both out and over a short period of time it successfully ate the majority of the fringing from around the bottom of our new sofa. She fed the thing on the finest bran flakes so it is a puzzle as to why it should want to subject its digestive system to sofa fringing. It did not pay to stand about too long in the house for fear of my trouser bottoms suffering the same fate. Purely as an act of revenge I considered eating it. I have seen them served up in Peru and are supposed to taste a bit like chicken, the drawback being they have a million tiny bones which is the only reason little 'piggy' did not end up on a plate. Carol took the hint and got rid of it only to replace 'piggy' with a mentally deranged dog called Jumbo that spent much of the day gnawing an unattractive frilly edge along the bottom of the kitchen cupboards. In all likelihood Jumbo would also have gone for the sofa fringing except 'piggy' had only left a dozen or so strands hanging and it was really not worth the bother. The thing is Jumbo was not quite like other dogs for he was part-dog and part-blockhead, but mainly blockhead. I did feel some pity towards Jumbo and tried to give him the benefit of the doubt, because if he did possess any brains, which is questionable then he would have known that the name Jumbo is normally reserved for elephants, so presumably he was suffering from an identity crisis from day one! In an effort to curb his boredom I brought him a massive knuckle bone which given its size could well have come from a fossilised Iguanodon. I was working on the theory that Jumbo might just break most of his teeth while crunching his way through the bone and a gummy dog would be far less destructive; and surely even the most simple-minded dog would quickly realise the negativity of sucking on the door of a kitchen cupboard. My cunning plan backfired. The thing was he persisted in hauling the bone up the stairs so he could grind away on it at the head of the stairs and every time I took it back down he would drag it back up. Inevitably I came out of the bathroom one morning with my head in a towel drying my hair (I was still possessively hanging onto a few remaining strands) when I tripped over the dog lying in his usual place at the top of the stairs and banged my head on a wall. This was never going to be a good start to the day. I rallied myself and in my anger cursed Jumbo and lashed out at him with my foot. He speedily side-stepped and my bare foot came into contact with the very hard and unforgiving knuckle bone. I feel sure I heard my toes snap as a blinding pain shot through my foot and I wanted to pass out on the spot. Idiot dog Jumbo had quickly got the measure of the situation and scampered down the stairs like lightening where he sat at the bottom with his tongue lolling to one side with an expression on his face that suggested he was not too sure of his next move, or mine. Wincing in pain I let fly. "You idiotic, half-witted, brainless waste of space. I'm sick of you and this b….y bone" whereupon I picked it up and flung it down the stairs hoping to possibly knock him out, or at least knock some sense into his thick skull. Fate of course, as we all know sits patiently in the wings waiting for opportunities like this to play its card and on this particular occasion it allowed the bone to bounce down the stairs, launch into the air and smash through the glass panel of the front door. "Now look what you've made me do, you stupid, stupid dog!" I bellowed, enraged by the damaged front door and distraught at my throbbing foot. The pain and the anguish were too much to bear at this time of the day and I was unable to decide whether to sit down and cry, or stagger downstairs and kill the dog. In the end I did neither, but the door repair proved to be an expensive piece of folly. Whoever was on 'fate' duty that particular day caught me again almost twenty years later in similar circumstances when I was living in Cornwall. I happened to glance out of my studio window in time to witness my middle son Lawrence who was very young at the time merrily slashing the tops off a clump of daffodils with a tennis racquet. Enraged I stormed outside, berated him severely, snatched the racquet and flung it hard down on the ground only to see it rise up into the air and smash its way through the rear window of our caravan parked in the yard. "Look what you've made me do, you stupid, stupid boy!" I yelled. Both of us still have a laugh about that incident to this day as he remembers it well, yet he still persists in saying it was entirely my fault. Kids!

Unfortunately, Carol's love of animals tended to be a little misplaced at times. On the few instances my parents came for a meal, my father found he was dealing with a two-edged sword for on the one hand he liked my wife's cooking very much but not, alas, her after dinner habits. He was a very fastidious man in the area of hygiene and was repulsed by the fact that Carol would collect all the plates from the table and put them on the floor for Jumbo to lick clean. As far as he was concerned each time he finished his meal all he imagined emblazoned across the plate was 'Welcome to Gastroenteritis' or perhaps as a change he might see 'Welcome to Hepatitis A'. I have to agree with him. Dogs licking plates is not a habit to encourage, after all I would not wish to eat my meal from a dog's bowl. Would you? My poor father always seemed to get the short straw for on spasmodic visits to see my bed-ridden great grandmother he was always subjected to the same old ritual heaped upon him by my well-meaning aunt Rosie. Great granny always kept a bottle of Port beneath her bed which in itself was off-putting and which my aunt Rosie always dragged out for my father's benefit. Aunt Rosie insisted despite my father's protests to the contrary that he should have a glass. The glass itself was usually unclean looking, a fact not entirely overlooked by my aunt Rosie who always breathed heavily into it before wiping it on her pinafore. The pinafore, it has to be said did not seem to have been washed within living memory, so once again as far as my father was concerned the words barely discernable in his mind's eye through the grimy pinafore spelt out, 'Welcome to Gastroenteritis'. I bet she had a back-up 'pinny' somewhere in a drawer that said 'Welcome to Hepatitis A'. No wonder he hated visiting and much preferred to stay at home.

September was upon me and with a flurry of hand-shaking, well-meaning messages and of course the ubiquitous round of fresh cream cakes (not bought by me this time) I said goodbye to the world of work and stepped into the world of college and student life. I enrolled for my course on photography and filled in a grant application form. This all took place at the new college of Art and Technology on Kedleston Road where I entered as a 'mature' student because I was twenty-one, whereas most other students were probably eighteen having just left school. At least I had had a shot at the real world and could feel slightly smug about my fellow students being utterly oblivious of the fresh cream cake ordeal that would face many of them later in life. My grant when it appeared was the grand sum of £112 a year, so that rapidly dispelled any ideas I may have had about living the high life and fanciful photographic weekends in Acapulco. I was going to miss my salary. The students in my year were for the most part attired in scruffy jeans and sloppy tops with a variety of adornments as they tried to express their individuality. I normally wore 'needle cord' trousers and jacket which was more in the style of David Bailey, or Peter Wyngarde, or maybe it was just me. One of the lads was from an African state and had stinking rich parents and was never short of money, unlike everyone else, and he arrived at college sporting a Hasselblad camera and smoking

Du Maurier cigarettes while we were always on the scrounge for anything resembling a cigarette. Not surprisingly he was a tad unpopular for much of the time due to his unwillingness to share his smokes accompanied by an air of general arrogance that did him no favours. Another student who was a little older than most came from Germany and proved himself to be quite irritating as he insisted on using the same enlarger every time he was in the print room. 'Thisz isz mine enlarger, I am uszin' thisz one alvaze' he would bellow if he came into the room and found someone else printing with it. He normally earned himself a mouthful of abuse, but either way we were left in no doubt that when he turned up in the print room the Third Reich had arrived and we had all better 'Snell! Snell! Vee hav vayzs of makin' you move, ya?' The students in the years above us were in general a pretty amicable bunch, especially the lads who immediately eyed up the new contingency of female recruits deciding whichever girl they thought they should first try it on with in the darkroom.

Extra-curricular activities were common place particularly in the film processing booths where you could lock yourself in to develop a film along with developing your modus operandi on a willing girl. Down one side of the room ran a long sink of temperature controlled tanks of processing chemicals, while on the other side was a table for unloading cameras, or as was often the case, a suitable top for unloading a nubile young girl for a search and plunder mission in the dark as your film developed. Why do I get the feeling I might be hanging myself here? The rooms were small and stuffy at the best of times, but to enter one where the previous occupants had enjoyed themselves then the reeking nauseous cocktail of sweaty carnal lust and acrid chemicals invaded the nostrils before you knew what had hit you. Actually, these rooms reminded me of the record booths in town where you could request a record of your choice and then listen to it in privacy. These booths were often lined with pegboard (perforated hardboard) and usually had the malodourous vapours of Brylcream, Old Spice aftershave and cigarette ash, or if it had been occupied by girls then a lung-clogging pong of hairspray, talcum powder and Evening in Paris might assault your nostrils and all but floor you! Listening to the 'Sounds of the Sixties' could be a hazardous, life-threatening way to spend a Saturday afternoon. Distractions at college were normally due to the female genre like the slim, sensual dark-haired girl of Mediterranean origin who carried before her a pair of very sizeable, eye-watering breasts the likes of which I had never before seen. Now she was a distraction and she knew it. It would be deemed as a high-risk situation if she sashayed past when you were glazing prints as the extremely hot, slowly revolving glazing drum was not a machine you would wish to catch your clothing in, or worse a bodily appendage thus making concentration paramount, on the machine that is, not the breasts. After all third degree burns on a flattened bodily protuberance sporting a high gloss finish might be a tad embarrassing to explain at A&E. The thing is, however you wish to present it, copulation, bonking, screwing, porking, nooky, rumpy-pumpy or just plain old it; sex seemed to be happening almost all of the time between students, students with tutors and even tutors with tutors. I am surprised that anyone ever had enough energy left to get anything done!

One of the good aspects of the photography course was that we were always being sent out to do projects. Our very first project, presumably so the tutors could assess the measure of us was to go out and take photographs of anything below knee level. Predictably, there was a plethora of pictures showing drains, bases of lamp-posts, rotting door bottoms, milk bottles on doorsteps and a shot someone had taken of their own feet. Luckily there were no dwarves on the course as this would have narrowed it down considerably for them. I used my own camera which I had saved up for while still at work. It was a Praktica and although lacking the class and style of say a Nikon, it was nevertheless a real trusty workhorse and virtually indestructible and to prove this point the following is precisely what happened to mine several years later. I was photographer for Lancaster University Speleological Society's expeditions to a massive cave system they had discovered in the mountains of the Picos de Europa in northern Spain. On this particular occasion I had initially gone into the first part of the system to haul all my photographic gear to a convenient spot. This included boxes of PF1, PF5 and the large PF60 and PF100 flash bulbs, (a bit of technical information for those of you who may remember such things) flash guns, connecting leads and my Praktica camera which was housed in a specially adapted ammunition box which was immensely sturdy and not easy to open. The flashbulbs which now days would be considered antiques were coated in blue plastic that gave the correct daylight level for colour photography and also prevented hot glass flying everywhere when they were fired. After one had been fired the coating crackled in the heat and gave off a smell like a burnt Werther's Original. The idea had been to re-enter the cave the following day and haul the gear further on after some shots of the main stream passage. However, during the night the heavens opened and it rained and rained and rained. I was camped outside the cave in the confines of the gorge and next day it continued to rain and rain and rain to the extent that the water level was filling the gorge and there was nowhere I could go. By day three I was forced to move out from my precarious position beneath a dripping rock shelter just above the swollen river and trudge back up the sides of the near vertical gorge as lightening flashed all around, at one stage striking a rock face above me. I had a large metal gas cylinder in my backpack at the time. Worried? You bet I was! Anyway, several weeks later when I was back at work in England I got a phone call to meet one of the guys from the expedition in a nearby pub at lunchtime. When I got there he told me it was over a week before the water had subsided sufficiently to get into the cave and find that a lot of their equipment had been swept away as indeed had mine, except for one thing. Someone had spotted my distorted ammunition box irretrievably jammed down a narrow crevice with its lid torn off by the ferocity of the flood water. Reaching into the box they discovered my camera, rather wet and a little battered around the edges. When it dried out the shutter release system still worked so in essence it would still take photographs. Now that is what I call a robust camera.

To further encourage our unquenchable enthusiasm at college we were allowed at weekends to take home very expensive studio cameras, tripods and flash equipment. One particular weekend I borrowed a 5x4 plate camera and a Bowens studio flash outfit, and in a mate's sports car we headed north of Buxton to an abandoned tunnel I knew that was filled with amazing formations from delicate thin straw stalactites to hefty gleaming white columns. The entire tunnel was coated in a white crust because it seemed to have been built beneath some kind of lime tip which meant the formations consisted mainly of lime and not the usual and more solid calcite or aragonite of a real cave. The back of the tunnel had collapsed and was thigh deep in water with a thin translucent skin covering its surface. The thin skin should have been sufficient to ring alarm bells, but sadly it failed to register anything such was my eagerness to capture all before me. For a couple of hours I happily sploshed about with my 'wellies' full of freezing cold water and my legs devoid of all feeling. How I wished my legs had stayed that way. 'If only I'd known' what was coming. We both finally emerged outside where I emptied out my boots and my mate who had wisely kept out of the water helped me carry all the gear back to his car. As we motored along the road feeling pleased with ourselves I suddenly became aware that my ankles began to itch, sting and then burn as though they were immersed in boiling water. Gritting my teeth I cautiously removed both socks and discovered that my feet, ankles and lower leg were blood red and seemed to be missing a layer of skin. The pulsating pain became unbearable as the heavily laden lime water, for I now realised that was what it had been, continued to eat into my legs. Right then I would have paid good money to anyone we might have passed on the road who may have been carrying a chain saw or an axe and was willing to cut off both my legs, but typically, there is never a chainsaw murderer or crazed axe man around when you need one. When we arrived at my house I hobbled out of the car, dragged myself upstairs, half-filled the bath with water, stepped in and howled. My mate told Carol what had happened and immediately drove away leaving me to my fate. She overflowing with sympathy and concern told me I was a silly beggar and should have known better. By now I was past caring for I was in blinding agony, trouser-less and propping myself against the wall as my feet and legs turned to liquid lava. Somehow, and it is really all a bit of a blur now I hauled myself out of the bath crawled across the floor on my hands and knees and climbed onto the bed where I heroically covered my screamingly painful wounds in Vaseline and quietly awaited my fate. I did not have to wait long for fate quickly sought me out in the shape of pea-brained Jumbo who up until now had been shut in the kitchen but who was now racing upstairs at breakneck speed. Even before it happened the ensuing scenario somehow played in slow-motion through my mind as I shouted, "Don't let the dog out! Don't let that stupid d…!" But of course I shouted in vain. In a split second Jumbo bounded through the doorway, leapt into the air wearing an 'I'm so pleased to see you master' expression on his gormless face and landed right on top of my feet. I died an excruciating death. Everything went black after that, although I feel sure I remember a very close-up view of the ceiling followed by cracking my head on the wall as I landed back on the bed. Jumbo assumed it was playtime and continued to scratch away at the duvet, an unclear image seen through watery eyes of a wagging tail, his backside up in the air with flailing legs digging maniacally in an attempt to get at the remains of my feet. In the half-conscious vagueness that followed, as I lay paralysed with pain I heard a far off voice calling the dog and felt a weight lift off my legs as the imbecilic Jumbo was dragged back downstairs. I wanted to cry over the senseless agony I was in. I think I probably did before drifting off to sleep. Apart from necessary traumatic trips to answer the call of nature I never left my bed for the next three days with only my mind to exercise. The thing is that over a lifetime I reckon I have organised much of my life when lying in bed and thinking things over, which is no doubt responsible for the fact that I am really bad at sleeping. Most nights tend to follow a familiar format of, I think, I sleep, I wake, I think, I sleep, I wake and so on and so on until it is time to get up, whereupon I fall asleep and do not want to get up. Samuel Johnson once wrote rather sagely that 'The happiest part of a man's life is what he passes lying awake in bed in the morning'. For me thinking in bed has always been a very beneficial pastime and much has been achieved. However, if by some strange quirk of fate I should happen to awake one morning and discover I was sharing my bed with Kelly Brook or Ellie McPherson, then I would find myself 'passing' some very 'happy' and pleasantly distracting thoughts and it would have nothing to do with who is going to get up and make the tea!

Despite everything I had suffered on that fateful trip the pictures turned out well and I decided to devote more time to cave photography as there were few people in the sixties who were attempting the subject with any degree of professionalism, so it was a fairly open field. My next cunning move was to get some money out of the student union by forming a college caving club which would require cash for equipment. In order to pull this off it necessitated me going before the student committee and convincing them that my scheme would be an added bonus to college life for anyone interested in underground exploits, which of course would be carried out as a very serious speleological procedure (Yeh, right!) for which I would be responsible. I omitted to mention the eagerly anticipated riotous weekends to be spent in various Peak District pubs. They took the bait, handed over some money which I spent on two Electron caving ladders and two hundred feet of Ulstron rope and the 'EREBUS' caving club got underway. I came up with the name Erebus for in Greek mythology he was a primordial deity representing the personification of darkness (I knew you knew that anyway). A poster on the college notice board made it all look bona fides. This announced our first trip to Carlswark cavern for anyone who really had nothing better to do with their time on a Saturday afternoon. The main idea of the club was to enable me and a friend called Richie who was a year above me on the same course, to skive off when we could on the pretence of taking cave pictures and have a good day underground, so naturally we were a bit put out when a few people put their names down for the first trip. A motley crew turned up that Saturday, ill prepared, ill equipped and for the most part unwelcome apart from a young girl called Kate who got special attention when it came to tying the rope around her waist as she was well endowed in the upper regions, a fact which needed to be taken into consideration in the interest of safety that promoted unavoidable close contact. We pre-laddered a mine shaft for exit later then led everyone around to the cave entrance proper. Richie and I were the only ones properly equipped with miner's headlamp packs and helmets. Others wore building-site safety hats except for one clown who wore his motorcycle crash helmet which prevented him from hearing anything that was being said to him. Predictably, every time he took off his helmet to hear what was being said to him he banged his head on the roof which amused us greatly, though he failed to see the funny side of it. We shinned up a narrow rift, walked along a passageway, crawled through a half-sump and made it to the end without incident until somebody admitted they had lost their torch. Somebody else desperately needed to go to the lavatory complaining that all the grunting and squeezing had forced his bowels into action (reason enough to make sure you were ahead of him on the way out) and Kate, who was rather underdressed and appeared to be in the early stages of hypothermia. There were a few suggestions put forward for warming her up, all of which were totally indecent, agreeable but indecent, so we resorted to getting her back to the surface as soon as possible. For an introduction to caving I think it was fairly safe to say it had not been a huge success and Richie and I were determined to discourage any further interest by any other students which would allow us to use the college equipment for our own ends whenever we felt the need.

It seems that the need arose quite often and the two of us would skive off from college in the middle of the week on the pretence of taking photographs for an end of term project. It was on one such trip that found the pair of us downing a couple of pints and playing lunchtime darts in the Duke of York near Flagg. Afterwards we came across an old mine shaft and dropped the ladder down. I descended first and the further down I went the narrower it appeared to get until there was little room for manoeuvre. Looking down I spotted a dead sheep jammed beneath me in the shaft looking very much past its 'sell by date' for Sunday lunch. Consequently, it left me with no option but to step on it. It was a bit like standing on memory foam as my feet slowly sank into its body, whereupon it let out a long, loud 'Baaaaahh' which for a dead sheep scared the hell out of me and almost made me wet my wet suit. I assume what had happened was that gases in its swollen body had been compressed by my weight and forced out over its vocal chords and out of its mouth for it was most definitely dead. As a sense of relief flooded over me so did an overwhelming stench of putrid decomposed intestines, organs and goodness knows what else. Trapped in the confined space I forgot all about wetting myself as I now badly wanted to wretch. I stepped back onto the ladder and the sheep gave a barely audible sigh as I escaped the foul air polluted with 'essence of fetid sheep' heading quickly for the surface and fresh air. We never did explore that particular shaft.

You would think that an experience of that nature would occur only once in a lifetime, and yet a decade or so later providence deemed that I would find myself in an even more ghastly situation. I was part of an expedition in the Picos mountains in northern Spain and had befriended a local man called Basilio who had spent time living with his oversized wife in a trailer somewhere in America. He spoke a good form of pidgin English and had developed a habit of ending most of his sentences with the expression 'son of a gun' an Americanism he should have left there along with his wife which he had done. Anyway he told me of a cave he knew that had not been explored, so we set off down the side of a tremendously steep gorge thick with walnut trees and scrubby bushes with Basilio's moth-eaten looking dog in tow. The entrance to the cave was an unbelievable tight squeeze but proved no obstacle for the dog that shot in ahead of us. After what must have been comparable to getting into an undersized corset we found ourselves in a tunnel and were able to crawl along and explore the system. Some twenty minutes or so later the tunnel ended with a deep shaft in the floor which barred any further progress, so we turned and headed back along the low passageway that only just allowed an ungainly, spread-eagled arms and legs crawl. All was going well until we stopped to admire a cluster of crystals in the roof when the silence was suddenly broken by a splashing, spurting sound from up ahead. I bet you can almost guess what is coming next, and yes you are right, it was Basilio's mangy dog with its back arched and tail straight out discharging a fetid flood of faecal slop that cascaded across the floor of the narrow passageway. In such a confined space the stench was overpowering and it was all we could do to stop ourselves vomiting. We desperately needed to get out of the cave, yet somehow we had to pass over the ever-increasing pool of steaming brown sewage which even the dog had now deserted and was nowhere to be seen. There was no other option but quickly and delicately manoeuvre our way over it and as I did so my eyes were drawn to a writhing heap of black worms in the middle of it all which the dog had deposited on the floor. That dog was seriously unhealthy and I have to say that neither of us felt exactly 'tip-top' after that underground venture. Outside we spotted the dog skulking about in the scrub looking both guilty and afraid as if it instinctively knew that a death sentence was in the offing if either of us ever got our hands on him. In the world of thespians they always say you should avoid acting with children and animals and I now extend this philosophy to caving, especially if the animal is a dog with the canine equivalent of dysentery!

Back in the Peak District Richie and I continued with our alleged underground photography trips in college time and on another occasion went to explore Mouldridge mine entering it from a shaft on the hilltop. We crawled around a few tunnels until we came to a dead end where we found lying on the floor some glistening tubes in peeling brown paper. I picked one up and it felt moist in my hand and by the light of my lamp I could just make out the word Dynamite.

"Oh s…! These are old sticks of Dynamite" I exclaimed.

"B….y, hell!" blurted Richie, "and they're all sweaty."

"Isn't that bad news?" I asked nervously. "Aren't they supposed to be very unstable if they're old and sweaty?" Suddenly I felt very unstable and sweaty myself. "What shall I do with it? "What if it goes off when I put it down?"

"Well, you're the one holding it" which were Richie's last words on the matter as he sped back down the tunnel quicker than a ferret up a drainpipe. I sat for a short time, or maybe it was weeks, gazing at the potentially lethal object in my hand and some thought drifted through my mind about curiosity killing a cat. I imagined a blinding white flash, an ear-splitting BOOM, and when the smoke had cleared the wall of the tunnel dripping with minced meat and black fragments of wet-suit that had formerly been me! My wife would not be best pleased as my dinner would be going cold. My mother would be quite vexed and wag her finger in a knowing manner while mumbling something about how she was forever telling me to stick to collecting match-box labels as nobody ever got themselves killed with a match-box label; in fact only half-witted Jumbo would carry on with his life as though nothing had happened. Not much to show for an obituary. However, as things turned out I gingerly put the stick of Dynamite back with the others and the two of us celebrated the joys of being alive in the Pig of Lead at Cromford. Richie refused to pay for all the drinks despite me pointing out that he had deserted me in my hour of need. His reply was that he saw no reason for two of us being blown to smithereens when one would do just as well. B…..d!!

Life at college was generally predictable as I spent my time photographing things, printing things and attending the Friday afternoon 'crit' sessions where we all exhibited our creative efforts for everyone to see and then 'slag-off' everyone else's work except our own. Then the tutors would chip in with their professional opinions normally culminating in the fact that none of us had really produced much and we should get out of bed earlier, stop wasting time and cut down on the fraternising with each other (this was rich coming from one tutor who regularly bedded a girl in my class) for at this rate nobody would be passing any exams. On the whole they were fairly encouraging comments that few people took any notice of as these same comments rolled out week after week, term after term. We still found the history of art lessons last thing on a Friday afternoon too boring to attend and business studies were equally as unpopular; and the lecturer who mainly read from the pages of the photography manual we had all been made to purchase at the start of the course we found both tedious and sleep inducing. Having to learn all the constituents of different developers proved to be just too much and in my opinion as a one-time professional photographer in the real world, provided you knew what the end result was in relationship to whatever film you were processing who cares what chemicals were in the developer. It was not as if you were going to mix your own, because you simply ordered whatever you required from Kodak and just added water. Quite a lot of litho-film was used at college on the pretence of being 'creative' as it reduced a normal full tone picture to just black and white and the interest lay in which way the half tones would go. I produced such a rendition with a picture of the columnar portico of the ruined Sutton Scarsdale Hall which was so successful that I was able to sell a number of prints, thus boosting my flagging income. Buoyed-up by my success I followed this same technique with what appeared to be a naked woman rising from a laundry basket. You may like to keep soiled underwear in your laundry basket, but give me a naked lady any day and to hell with the weekly washing. The lady in question worked in an office at my wife's solicitors and was a slim, willowy, gorgeous looking girl with long flowing blonde hair who was not at all fazed about being partly stuffed into a laundry basket. The session took place on a Saturday afternoon and I had borrowed all manner of equipment from college which I set up in the bedroom at home. She arrived on the dot and duly stripped down to her very scant black underwear as ostensibly that was as far as she was prepared to go. To make her appear naked in the harsh contrasting light I had to reduce her underwear further which she happily agreed to and an interesting and provocative ten minutes followed with me and a roll of sticky tape. The lithographed picture I made from this session was transferred into calendars which sold, not surprisingly much more successfully than my previous effort. The bottom line was that I needed more funds and consequently I had no alternative but to take on a summer job, so I became a butcher.

There was a slight trace of butchering in the blood (no, I did not come from a long line of mass-murderers) because my father as a young lad had worked for Morleys a butcher at the end of Sadler Gate. I can remember as a child going into the shop with my mother with its white tiled walls, all manner of carcasses hanging from hooks and the now lost aroma of meatiness and fresh sawdust scattered over the floor. My father's duties included preparing some of the products, serving customers and making deliveries on his butcher's bike complete with a large wicker basket on the front. On one occasion he was told to deliver an order immediately to Kedleston Hall for it seemed that Lady Scarsdale was in desperate need of a pork sausage or two and could turn a tad awkward if she was kept waiting, so my father was sent on his hefty butcher's bike along the road to the hall. I have no idea how long it took him to get there but he did arrive and pulled up on the gravel in front of the impressive stepped main entrance. Within seconds an upstairs window was flung open and an angry man dressed in black bellowed at my father, 'You boy! Where the devil do you think you are? Deliveries are around the back of the house and be quick about it.' My father responded by blowing a raspberry at him before cycling quickly around to the kitchen door where he handed over the sausages and sped off at high speed before the butler, or whoever he was caught hold of him and clipped him about the ear for being cheeky to his elders. I remember visiting Kedleston Hall as a young lad, but not on a butcher's bike. It was a grey, overcast Sunday afternoon and long before the National Trust had taken it on, and Lady Scarsdale herself was on the door taking the ticket money from the public. This was even before Ken Russell's film *'Women in Love'* saw Alan Bates relate with impropriety the vulgar technique of eating a fig with its sensual secrets being compared apparently by the Italians to a female's yoni! Had her Ladyship eavesdropped on that particular conversation it may have caused her to get a tad hot under the collar and propel her towards the 'blower' to urgently request that Morleys immediately send over that cheeky young lad with more sausages. For those of you of a more recent generation the use of the word 'blower' refers to a telephone originating from the old speaking tubes often found in country houses, but in particular on ships, linked for example from the ship's bridge to the engine room. The captain would remove a bung and blow down the tube which had a whistle on the other end thus alerting the engine room. They could then speak to each other by alternatively holding the end to one ear or shouting down the tube. Simple, effective, but rather limited. It would not for example work if you were in Derby and wished to speak to aunt Florrie in Nottingham. You would merely shout yourself speechless, have a terribly sore throat and put yourself into a state of exhaustion and exasperation.

My father in his youth seemed to quickly take umbrage over the slightest of things, as happened on another occasion when a snooty women customer got shirty with him over something or other in the butcher's shop. When she came to collect a prepared chicken later on in the week my father handed it over having purposefully left its insides intact. Unbelievable as it now seems, she or someone in her household cooked the chicken without noticing. Now with things heating up and popping, and bursting, and seeping unmentionable liquids and matter into the carcass it seems only reasonable that she returned to the butchers shop in an extreme state of tetchiness and threw a tantrum in front of Mr Morley. He in turn eyed my father with suspicion but the case against him was never proven. My wife, a professional chef remarked that anyone who cooks a chicken totally unaware that it still contains all its innards must be a complete cretinous numbskull. Harsh words indeed, but then you probably know how 'prima donna' and critical chefs can be these days. Some form of revenge normally seeks you out in one way or another and you get your comeuppance as happened to my father when years later during the war he was working in Swindon and stayed in a boarding house with some fellow workers. For dinner one evening the landlady produced the world's worst stew that looked both unappetising and apparently uneatable and left him wondering just what she had made it from. She collected the almost full plates in an unnerving silence. Next day at work as lunchtime came around and everyone was hungry having been a dinner down from the previous night, they opened their lunchboxes only to discover that the canny landlady had given them all cold stew sandwiches!

My actual initiation into the bloodied world of raw meat came via my brother-in-law Gerfried who was a master sausage maker. He had escaped from eastern Germany because the Russians were getting a bit possessive and silly and started building a very long garden wall with very few doors. This convinced Gerfried that he did not wish to be on the side making sausages for stroppy communists, so he upped sticks and fled. Now as escapes go his was nothing anywhere near as spectacular as say *The Great Escape* with Steve McQueen flying over the top of a fence on a motorbike, but nonetheless, I gather there were more than a few 'sweaty palm' moments before he got to England. He was now in charge of a meat preparation factory in Derby that serviced the needs of a chain of butcher's shops, but his presence as a German was not always accepted. Apparently one day he discovered a swastika drawn on the door of a refrigerator. I have to say that given the fact Gerfried was young, well-built and well versed in the art of pugilism, and had he been wielding a meat cleaver in one hand at the time then he would have been a formidable opponent, and whoever was responsible for the swastika was certainly pushing their luck and fortunate not to be seeing the inside of the meat mincer and viewing the world through a sausage skin!

I was taught how to correctly divide up a side of pig, and beef, and cut with the aid of a giant bandsaw, carcasses of frozen New Zealand lamb, press burgers and make sausages. The latter proved to be an eye-opener for the main maker of sausages was a doddery, curmudgeonly old boy called Ron who wore glasses with lenses thicker than those of the Hubble telescope, yet he still failed to see everything he was putting into the sausage meat grinder. Much of the meat came as cut-offs in plastic boxes from all the branch shops and could contain other things apart from meat like plastic price tags and cigarette ends which seemed to escape Ron's attention as he happily bunged the whole lot into the grinder. On the other hand, perhaps he thought the flavour of old fag ash and the crunchy bits of minced plastic would give the sausages an individuality that might prove popular with the public. For this reason alone the two pounds of free sausages we were given on a Friday along with our wages could be said to be both a bonus and a threat. It is not that I am particularly squeamish about these things for I have eaten both sausages and cheese in villages high in the mountains of northern Spain that contained little wriggly maggots. The locals said these maggots were not harmful and simply tasted of the hot spicy sausage that both they and I were eating, and likewise with the cheese. Something tells me that spicy maggot and cheesy maggot is unlikely to catch on big time even as flavours for crisps. As for plastic shards and fag ash, I think not. My introduction to the sausage machine was quite nerve-racking as within seconds of it being switched on I was confronted with a flailing pink tentacle of a one-armed octopus that grew longer by the second and which I somehow had to grab hold of and wrestle to the ground. Once I had shown it just who was boss around here and had it under control and twisted into individual sausages, there came the tricky business of knotting all the pink, slimy things into manageable bunches. As both a climber and a caver I knew a bit about knotting ropes and could manage a reef knot, a pole hitch and a bowline (something about a rabbit, a hole and a tree) and once managed a double sheep-shank, but knotting a sausage was a whole new experience. I think attempting a double sheep-shank of sausages would be a bit showy as well as difficult to say without spraying saliva everywhere. My early attempts were lacking to say the least and I hoped that at some time in the future I would not find myself dangling over a rock face tied to the end of a string of sausages I had knotted myself! Unlikely

I admit, but it was just a passing thought. Apart from an attractive young girl in the office who I once took out at lunchtime for a drink to discuss her views on the merits of sausages and beef burgers (I don't know how I can write such a blatant lie) the only other break from the monotony of work was in complete contrast to spending a lunchtime in a pub with a desirable girl. This was when the offal lorry arrived although the pungent, nostril-wrenching smell normally arrived well before the lorry had backed into the loading bay. It was an open-backed affair containing large oil drums awash with animal organs in varying states of putrescence that slopped about releasing an unforgettable miasma that assaulted the nostrils and invaded the entire factory. Only the office staff escaped the humming pong safe behind the windows of their room and appeared to take a sadistic delight in seeing the likes of me rolling a drum of rank organs and entrails stew onto the back of the lorry. When I look back I realise that life comes with a multiplicity of repugnant smells and I could very easily compile a list, but that might be going a bit too far. After a number of years my brother-in-law gave up the factory and in time headed north, invaded Scotland armed with crates of German wines and bombarded them with Bratwursts, Knackwursts, Leberwursts and Frankfurters, thus showing the Scots that the humble haggis was not the only edible thing running about in a skin.

Another holiday earner was working for a friend of my wife who managed a television rental shop in East Street which I think may have been Rediffusion. Anyway, I did some advertising graphics for the shop window and he then got me a job working with a few girls in the television repair call centre. Here I sat alongside three girls waiting for complaints to come in, which were more often than not from irate customers who seemed to regard their need to watch television as vital as a blood transfusion. I developed my own opener 'Good afternoon, and what is the nature of the fault?' which apparently the girls found amusing. One day I was handed a call from one of the girls who thought it would be good for a laugh to see me deal with what turned out to be an extremely truculent man. Innocently I took the call.

"Good afternoon Sir, and what is the nature of the fault?" I asked.

"Fault! I'll tell you wot's the fault mate, the b....y telly caught fire that's wot an' I've chucked it into the front garden" yelled a voice down the phone.

"Okay, well I'll send a repair man out as soon as possible, but he may be a couple of hours" I replied hoping to placate him a little.

"A couple of hours! A couple of hours! That's no b....y good is it? If the missus don't get to watch *Coronation Street* there'll be hell to pay, I'm tellin ya."

"I'm sorry but I..."

"We wants a new telly that's wot, cos we ain't payin' good money to have a telly burnin' in the garden, so get us a new telly now!" he demanded angrily.

By now the girls were sniggering behind their hands as clearly I was getting out of my depth, and it was only my second day there.

"So wot ya gonna do mate, send us a new telly?" he continued aggressively.

"I'll get straight onto the engineers and tell them it's an emergency and the decision will rest with them" I answered.

"What decision eh? There ain't no decision to make is there, cos if my missus don't get to watch *Coronation Street* an' don't get to watch *This is Your Life* then there'll be World War Three 'appenin' so the only decision I'm interested in is a new telly."

"I'm afraid that issuing a new set is beyond my jurisdiction and the best I c....."

"Yeah, well wots your name then pal? Give us your name an' I'm gonna drop you right in it mate? So wot you got to say about that then? Get me the manager" he bellowed.

"Just one moment Sir I'll hand you over" and seizing the opportunity to be rid of this moron I thrust the phone into the hand of the nearest girl and said, "He wants to speak to the manager… you're move I think". I have no idea what the outcome was in this particular case but it did put a stop to the girls giving me belligerent customers and we all got on a lot better after that incident. I quickly realised how awful the job really was and I left before the second week was out for I was bemused how much television appeared to rule some people's lives. Okay, I readily admit to watching *Dr Finlay's Casebook* and *The Forsyth Saga*, but little else held my attention and my life would have gone on just the same if I missed an episode, whereas the man I had to deal with seemed ready to kill if his wife's viewing was to be interrupted. Maybe she had threatened to kill him if he did not sort it out pronto. Who knows?

My final summer holiday job was at Reed Polyfilms on Raynesway which proved to be rather demanding on my grey cells for it involved stocktaking, which in turn involved mental arithmetic. Arithmetic and I never really got on too well. I was fine at doing mental, the arithmetic was the problem. The handful of us taken on to perform this scintillating task (believe me once you've seen one roll of polythene, you've seen them all...yawn) were given instruction on how to add figures quickly so we would not be wasting any time, or to be more precise, their time and their money. On reflection I rate it as the most boring and unrewarding thing up until then that I had ever done. It was probably as mind-numbing as being locked in a room and forced to listen to a loop-tape of the Smurfs singing *The Smurfs Theme Song* and that really would be extreme soul-destroying torment. The upside to all this was that it did put money in my pocket and I decided that some of it should go towards paying for a few driving lessons. I booked six lessons and after only six lessons I took my driving test. I really think my instructor should have known better, but he said nothing. I took the morning off from college and set out with an examiner. Now one of the things that had been drummed into my head was never to act on other driver's instructions as it could lead to an unprecedented accident which would be my fault. With this in mind I was driving along Duffield Road when the examiner told me to turn right. I indicated, positioned myself in the middle of the road and waited for a gap in the oncoming traffic. After a while a car stopped and flashed its lights and although I knew what this meant I remembered my schooling and thought to myself, 'You're not catching me out matey, I'm on a driving test' so I stayed where I was. He however was rather persistent and continued to flash his lights and then began waving his arms about. Smugly I sat there refusing to act upon his signals whereupon he finally gave up and roared past me shaking his head and mouthing something that in hindsight I realise was not at all complimentary. A dozen more cars drove by and then another stopped and flashed and I carried on doing what I thought to be the correct procedure. A quick glance at my instructor's stony face seemed to suggest that he was pondering on how to inform his family that in all probability he would be spending Christmas, still several months away, stuck in a car with an idiot in the middle of Duffield Road and to look out for us appearing on the next edition of a Street Map of Derby. I must confess that even I sitting there waiting for a suitable gap in the traffic noticed that time seemed to be slipping by and wished I had brought along a flask of tea and some sandwiches. A serenade of blaring horns both behind me and in front strongly suggested that things were getting a little out of hand and my examiner in an unmistakable tone that strongly implied 'You don't stand a cat in hells chance of passing this driving test' suggested in a rather facetious tone I thought, that I should turn right immediately as I was holding up an awful lot of traffic. It seems I could not do right for doing wrong and the other thing was he was absolutely right in predicting I would fail my driving test. Uncanny or what?

It would be the best part of another six years before I took another driving test by which time I was working in East Anglia and had bought myself an old canvas-top, Series 1 Land Rover which enabled me to get in some much needed practice between the weekly driving lessons. I would drive over to Bedford under legal supervision by a young lady friend on Saturday afternoon shopping sprees for both her and my wife. I was in essence merely a taxi driver. My actual driving lessons were taken during the winter months after work and of course, in the dark, which in this instance meant pitch black darkness because the Miner's Strike of 1972 was well underway and all street lighting remained off to conserve energy. Consequently, driving around the suburbs of Cambridge under these conditions added an extra challenge to my would-be skills as a learner driver and for much of the time I might just as well have been driving in a tunnel. The day of the test came as quite a shock for the route I was to take, although well practised, appeared before me for the first time in daylight and how totally different it all looked. Anyway, all went well and that lunchtime I drove back to work in my old Land Rover feeling pretty pleased with myself. The thing was with a driving instructor called Mr Luck I could hardly have failed.

One Enema too Far

I needed to busy myself out of college with other activities and clearly driving was not going to be one of them. I occasionally went climbing with Kev, but he now had a girlfriend who demanded that he spent as much of his free time clambering around her rather than the Peak District. As she was another of Carol's friends I decided they should accompany Kev and myself on one of our climbing days out in the hope that they might just enjoy the countryside, for neither of them seemed overly enthusiastic about the great outdoors. The scene was set for a Sunday train trip to Miller's Dale (return ticket cost 10/9d each, which is somewhere around 55p in today's money) with the four of us and hair-brained Jumbo in tow. Arriving at Miller's Dale station in the sunshine we alighted from the train, apart that is from Jumbo, who despite being on a leash managed to disappear down the gap between the platform and the carriage where he now hung, choking and spluttering. I dragged him out by the scruff of his neck and he seemed none the worse for his experience, or as was more likely, he was simply too stupid for it to have registered in what might possibly pass for a brain. In later life, I sometimes feel a sense of guilt about all the harsh and detrimental things I have said about poor old Jumbo especially in the pages of this book, but he did not seem to be like other dogs. I am not the sort of person who anthropomorphises animals and certainly not in Jumbo's case for I am sure he was a species unto himself and he would have given Darwin the run around had he tried to place Jumbo on the evolutionary scale! I cannot help thinking that even when Jumbo decided to hang up his leash for good he managed to get the next bit wrong. Instead of going to that 'Doggy Kennel' somewhere up in the sky, being a canine clod he took the wrong turn and ended up in another department wondering why all the inhabitants were smaller than him, had round furry faces, arched backs and sticky-up tails and spent the entire time hissing and spitting at him!

Our destination that day was Chee Dale and a rock wall near where the railway line bursts out of a tunnel, leaps across a narrow gorge and disappears quickly into another tunnel. Kev was excited about a new piton he had bought that had a blade no longer than my thumb-nail which he wanted to try out in a hair-line crack. The two girls walked along the riverside happily chatting to each other, while Jumbo insisted walking in the river looking as dozy as ever, but as a wet version. Arriving at the rock the girls sat down to watch the fun as Kev set off banging in pegs and clipping on his etriers (a short free swinging, three rung metal ladder) until he found a crack suitable for his new Lilliption peg which I have to admit rang out nicely as he hammered it in, thus suggesting a high degree of dependability. At this stage of the game he had tired himself out and roped down for a smoke followed by a coughing session, then an inhaler pumping session, and only then was he ready to belay me. I quickly reached his new pride and joy, clipped on my etrier, stood on it and watched as in slow motion the peg quietly bent downwards and effortlessly prised itself out of the crack. There was barely time to let out a string of expletives before I fell to the next peg below me which also popped out and not surprisingly so did the third one. I hit the ground and winded myself. The girls thought it was hysterical and could not stop laughing. Kev joined in until it brought on yet another coughing spasm followed by yet another inhaler pumping session, and Jumbo with his truly amazing inability to assess any situation correctly, bounded out of the river, up the bank, shook water all over me then started to attack my trouser leg. A sense of hopelessness descended over me and I felt I was coming to the end of an era. The girls could not see any point in coming out all this way just to fall off and Kev slowly exited the climbing scene as he was needed for other things by his wife to be. I was left to my own devices. I had spent the majority of my life in the Peak District and was not about to give it all up, so I foolishly took to climbing solo. Present day climbers simply go for it armed only with a bag of chalk dust, but in those distant days of my past I carried on with all the paraphernalia I was familiar with, namely ropes, pegs and etriers. I was not overly successful and still fell off and the ropes used to get in an awful tangle to the extent that I might have been better off trying to knit a Fair Isle jumper with them. The pleasure went out of it and I gave it up to concentrate on caving which I was far better at and of course in the dark I could not see how far I had to fall. Despite many severe situations I encountered during a few decades of caving and potholing both in this country and abroad, falling off was never one of them and neither was drowning. The latter will come as no surprise of course!

When I think back I realise just how liberal minded my parents were concerning the amount of freedom I was given and they never seemed to worry that I would not turn up at the end of a day out hanging off a rock-face, or descending a watery black hole. I think they must have adopted the concept that dangerous though these activities might seem, I could just as easily step out into the road and get run over by a bus. This particular saying is perhaps, less apt these days due to recessional cut-backs and infrequent bus services. The threat instead had been replaced by the silent killing machine that cruises unheard for the most part along the pavement of every town throughout the country. I refer of course to the menacing mobility scooter. You may well be familiar with the scenario where you step innocently out from a shop doorway, hear a dull thud and find yourself prostrate on the pavement with a tyre mark across your face; and through watering eyes you can just make out the blurred vision of what appears to be a small, plastic greenhouse on wheels rumbling away into the distance driven by a granny from hell who is away with the fairies and completely oblivious of your demise. On a rare occasion she might actually stop to bombard you with abuse for not looking where you were going, or worse, stop and lean over to ask if you are alright at the same time releasing an ill-fitting set of false teeth that land the wrong way around across the bridge of your nose, thus delivering the final ignominy to your already embarrassing situation. The world at times can seem to be a potty place to live in, but no doubt it will only become worse as man gets dafter with his inventions.

As both a student and a married man my social life tended to be two-fold. One weekend I might be heading for the Lake District to spend a freezing cold night cramped in the back of a Mini with three other college friends, climb Helvelyn in a snow storm, get half-frozen to death in the process (one lad only wore a tee-shirt, jeans and plimsolls! Stupid boy.) and arrive home feeling totally drained. 'Did you have a nice time? You look a bit tired.' enquires a cheery voice from the kitchen. 'Never mind its college in the morning'. Thank you wife for reminding me! Another weekend might be spent at a dinner party with Carol's associates eating mushroom vol-au-vents, avocado in vinaigrette and downing glasses of Irish coffee followed by tots of Bendictine or Tia-Maria. Now and then we would have friends over for a 'get-together' as happened one Saturday night when Carol decided to invite a lively young lad who worked at the same solicitors as she did. His name was Kevin Lloyd who at the time was just another clerk studying for his law examinations. We were not to know back then that he would become a household name starring as DC Alfred 'Tosh' Lines in the long running television series *The Bill*, although he did turn up at the house slightly the worse for drink which, unfortunately proved to be the deciding factor in his eventual demeaning demise. He was the only one at the gathering without a partner and became rather more boisterous as the evening wore on, until after a trip to the lavatory he left and I never saw him again. I only mention the lavatory because the following day I noticed he had written the name Kevin Keegan on the wall with a biro pen. Perhaps to an ardent fan that piece of scribble on lavatory wall might be worth something, even though by now it probably lies beneath several coats of emulsion paint.

In the sixties there was nearly always a party going on somewhere, and although I was not a particularly enthusiastic participant I did turn up at a few including one after I had spent all day underground. It was a wintery day and the Peak District lay beneath a good covering of snow. Three of us had collected a key from a nearby farm which was required to access the locked entrance to a mine. We trudged through the snow, opened the entrance and entered a tunnel. Caving in winter has the added bonus of being warmer underground than it is outside, but not to the extent that you can strip down to your underwear and lounge about drinking Pimm's No1 (well possibly in the old thermal Cumberland cavern at Matlock Bath) but it is noticeably warmer until you emerge later, wet and icy cold on the walk back through the snow. After we had done exploring we locked the entrance and headed back to the farm in darkness only to find the place deserted. We had collected the key from the back door but discovered there was nowhere to put it, so we went around to the front door and poked it through the letter box and went home. There was just time for a quick bath, a change of clothes and off for a bit of partying, boogying and drinking at a friend's house. As the night wore on a combination of fatigue and drink got the better of me and I fell asleep. I slumbered on during the taxi ride home and did not come around until seven thirty in the morning when I was violently awoken by the sound of somebody trying to smash down the front door, at least that is how it registered inside my pulsating brain. Carol went downstairs, opened the door and found herself confronted by two policemen who enquired as to whether or not I was at home. As she had just got out of a bed having spent the night with someone who vaguely resembled me, she was obliged to say yes. Half conscious, I staggered downstairs wondering what monstrous crime I may have committed while I had been sleeping.

"Mr Carter?" one of them enquired in an official manner.

"Yes" I replied sleepily.

"Were you caving in Knotlow mine yesterday?" he continued.

"Yes" I answered, still wondering what was coming next.

"And where were you last night?" he asked, fiddling with a button on his tunic.

"Partying at a friend's house."

"While you were partying Mr Carter" he went on in a tone that intimated that my partying had been a heinous act for which I would be placed before a firing squad at dawn, "the Cave Rescue" he continued, "were out searching for you in the mine because you did not return the key. Therefore they had to assume, despite there being three sets of footprints in the snow leading to the mine and the same three sets leaving, suggesting that in all likelihood you were not inside, they felt it their duty to enter the mine and undertake a search" he solemnly announced, obviously requiring an explanation.

"I put the key through the letterbox of the front door" I replied innocently. "There was nowhere else to leave it".

"I see" he said, writing something down in his notebook and trying to ignore Jumbo who had come to see what all the commotion was about and had positioned himself against the leg of the policeman and was doing something very doggy and disgusting around his crutch (his own crutch that is, not the policeman's).

"Have you got a licence for this dog?" he asked, glancing briefly at Jumbo with a look of distain.

"Oh, yes" chipped in Carol with all the confidence of a cross-examining lawyer, "It cost me seven shillings and sixpence. Would you like to see it?"

"Er, no thank you Madam, that won't be necessary."

Throughout the entire interview the second policeman never uttered a word, but kept on gazing around the room scrutinising everything as though he was trying to find a clue that would lead to my arrest and years of penal servitude. Finally, they both shuffled towards the front door, Jumbo passed wind and wisely scampered off into the kitchen and we went back to bed.

The outcome from all this was that the farmer never used his front door so it never occurred to him to check if the key was there. I cannot help feeling that it was all a bit over-dramatic considering there was no evidence to suggest that I or anyone else was still inside the mine. Perhaps the rescuers were a little over zealous on this occasion, but they are, nonetheless a first class organisation and cannot be faulted for their thoroughness that night. I blame the farmer for not looking more thoroughly, after all he only had two doors to check!

Suddenly, and probably for no apparent reason I decided I would try and get fit after spotting an advertisement in a newspaper. It was extolling the merits of a muscle-building course that was guaranteed by none other than Charles Atlas himself. Charles Atlas, real name Angelo Siciliano maintained he could transform any weedy individual into a beef cake with muscles on their muscles. I had always been a bit short on muscles.

I always had plenty of stamina but I was lacking in the bulging biceps department. My mother always used to say that we were 'Pharaoh's lean kind', an expression I never understood and one that still baffles me to this day. The advertisement ran along the lines of a comic strip depicting an emaciated guy sitting on a beach with his lady friend when a hulking bully comes along and kicks sand in their faces. What a bounder. At this point the weedy guy leaps to his feet and shouts 'Hey. Quit kicking sand in our faces!' Mr Muscles the bully turns on the scrawny weakling saying 'I'd smash your face only you're so skinny you might dry up and blow away.' Mr Muscles the bully was obviously not one to mince his words. However, several weeks later the former Mr Skinny is back on the beach as a new Mr Muscles and merrily punching the lights out of Mr Muscles the bully, much to the overwhelming delight of the new Mr Muscles girlfriend who is now all over him like a rash. The message was blindingly clear. If I did not want sand kicked in my face on a beach then I could take Charles Atlas at his word and after a couple of months training I to could go about punching people in the face on any beach. Well that all sounds perfectly reasonable to me! My initial reaction was that the nearest place to get sand kicked in my face was Skegness some seventy-seven miles away as the crow flies (Do crows really fly in straight lines?) which seemed a long way to go to suffer the humiliation of having sand kicked in my face, and equally so having to return there months later just to bash someone in the face; and did I really have to wear a very large pair of white underpants like Charles Atlas? I also had to address the question of how would I look with overdeveloped body parts that might be akin to something you could find hanging in any reputable butchers shop?

Undaunted I wrote out a cheque and sent off for the course which would arrive a part at a time. Part one duly arrived with a typed sheet of instructions along with some badly reproduced photographs showing Charles Atlas (and big pants) demonstrating various postures I needed to adopt in order to become a mountain of solid muscle onto which, according to the advertisement, a number of scantily clad women would cling rapturously next time I appeared on the beach. It would be worth the trip to Skegness for this fact alone, after all there was not much else at Skegness in those days especially if the tide was out, then you may as well be in a desert. The beach at Skegness with the tide out always brings to mind that old Tommy Cooper gag about the man driving across the Sahara desert who gets flagged down by a chap wearing a wet suit, flippers and a snorkelling mask, and he says to the driver, 'How far is it to the sea?' The driver pointing out of the car window says, 'About a thousand miles over there'. 'Oh' says the man, 'in that case I think I'll stay on the beach today.' Anyway, I started into part one of the course with boundless enthusiasm and after only a couple of mornings of gasping, wheezing, grunting, straining and sweating I could already feel a difference. My joints were racked with pain and I could barely move. Maybe I needed a big pair of white pants after all! I persevered week after week as more instructions arrived with more pictures of impossible contortions I was supposed to perform. They started to beg the question of whether or not I actually had all the requisite body parts to carry out these exercises, or had I been put together wrongly in my mother's womb. Had she read the kit instructions incorrectly and I had spent my life completely unaware that she had folded and stuck tab A into slot C instead of slot B? Bravely I carried on suffering abominable agonies of pulled muscles, twisted joints and knotted intestines until the day arrived when a certain course part popped through the letterbox explaining that in order to have a truly healthy body then it must be healthy inside as well as outside. Enter a picture of an eye-watering douche which I was required to purchase (special offer, only used once) to enable me to give myself a warm water enema. Somehow this did not rest easily on my mind. Somehow I had this vision of myself straddling the bath in the nip, rear end up in the air, pumping and squirting for England and my wife opening the bathroom door. Somehow I did not want to have to explain to her, rather sheepishly that it was not a fetish and I was quite happy with our sex life. You can see where I am coming from on this. To my way of thinking even just one enema would be one enema too far. This, I am afraid took the edge off the whole muscle building thing along with the fact that the weekly muscle measuring with a tape measure that lied to me because it gave out the same measurements week after week was sufficient to just make me go off the idea of rock hard muscles. I could feel a strong leaning towards abandoning the whole scheme, selling the thing to a mate at college and steering clear of beaches, at least for the foreseeable future. 'If only I'd known!' I could have saved myself some money and a near rupture.

Meanwhile back at college I was up to my ears in projects and trying to convince my tutors that I was in fact producing some work. During the 'foot and mouth' epidemic in1967 when movement around Derbyshire was strictly monitored, I was still able to get out and take some shots I wanted of Derbyshire pubs. This entailed using a studio plate camera to achieve the technicalities required of the picture and even more important was sampling the beer at each venue. The first port of call was the Derwent Hotel by the bridge at Whatstandwell, then on to Ye Olde Bear Inn, Pig of Lead (now a private Bed and Breakfast) Jug and Glass, Bull i' th' Thorn and ending up at the Cat and Fiddle which was perhaps, fortuitously closed for by now we were getting a tad tanked-up! All the photographs were taken in the snow and transferred into black-edged 20 x 16 black and white prints, which did not really fulfil the criteria of creative photographs and which my tutors did not particularly like even though they could not fault them technically. Anyway, my mate and I had a great day out, sampled a few fine ales and avoided getting 'foot and mouth'. However, I still have these one-off pictures to this day, some forty-five years on, so they are possibly of historic interest if only to the present pub owners. Offers anyone?

As the final twelve months hove into view the pace quickened and the panic intensified as there was much to do and I for one had not done enough. To encourage me and a girl called Kate (her of the first caving trip) we were given the opportunity to increase our versatility and skills by being taken by a tutor to his house in Coventry for the night. From here we went on to take pictures under difficult conditions of a rehearsal in progress at the Coventry theatre which would be a beneficial project for our final assessment, unless of course, we managed to foul up the rather critical exposures. Producing faint ghost images or pictures that seemed to have been taken in a coal cellar with no available light would not be beneficial to our final assessment. This was obviously going to be very serious stuff. The play being rehearsed starred Arthur Lowe of *Dad's Army* fame, and Dorothy Tutin of considerably less fame in a production of H. G. Wells story of *Anne Veronica*. For those of you not familiar with this tale then let me give you a brief resume that vaguely resembles the truth. Anne Veronica is a headstrong young woman who gets in a bit of a strop because her dad forbids her from going to a Saturday night 'bop' down the local Palais. This results in a good old barney with her sticking two fingers up at him and clearing off in a huff, after which she falls in love, gets frisked, joins the suffragettes and ends up in prison. You can clearly see she has become a bit of a wild card and not handling things too well and needs to seriously up her game. Upon her release she thrusts herself upon her former lover who is now married, but fails to stop our Annie V (the libertine!) from grabbing hold of him demanding, "I want you to kiss me. I want you. I want you to be my lover. I want to give myself to you. I want to be whatever I can to you. Is that plain?!!' so, no messing about there then. It is said that 'I want never gets' but not so with our Annie V (she really is a one!) who did, and after a lovely illegal honeymoon up a mountain in the Alps finds herself up the chuff, whereupon they all live blissfully happy ever after. How simply marvellous! Any questions? No, then I will carry on. Kate and I were told to move quietly, not create any distraction, so no bursting inflated paper bags or anything like that just for a bit of a laugh, and not to use flash. It was a peculiar experience creeping about the auditorium in the semi darkness watching and listening to those two actors in a pool of light on stage going through their lines in an almost empty theatre. It was an interesting session and next morning we were driven back to college to later watch Arthur Lowe and Dorothy Tutin slowly re-appear in a tray of developer in the darkroom.

On another occasion the same tutor took the pair of us to Castleton where I had arranged to meet the last of the Castleton rope makers, Herbert Marrison. Again it was a freezing cold snowy day (why am I always out in the depths of winter taking pictures?) when I met Herbert Marrison outside his workshop-cum-junk shed where it was said he could produce all manner of things from… well… all manner of things. He was dressed in an old trilby hat, a long tweed overcoat and wearing a pair of very dated horn-rimmed spectacles. We walked with him along a slushy footway between sturdy cottages to the gloom of the massive and impressive cavern entrance. He unlocked a gate and we entered the vast chamber with its weird and wonderful rope-walk, hand-cranked cord winders and ancient wooden structures on wheels that tensioned the hemp rope during the twisting process. In the freezing air my breath kept fogging the lens of my camera while the old rope-maker with cold gnarled fingers deftly spliced the ends of rope together in an instant, almost like magic as we stood in awe of his well-honed skills. Rope making had existed in Peak Cavern for centuries and in the past the cave was known as the *'Devil's Arse int'* Peak and had long been a dwelling place for not only the rope workers but also for an unsavoury bunch of vagabonds, miscreants and 'moon-men' which is an old term for gypsies, just in case you were thinking along the lines of Buzz Aldrin and other astronauts turning up to have a bit of a chin-wag about moon landings. Never have so many people walked, crawled and wriggled into the rear end of Old Nick with so much enthusiasm, curiosity and total disregard for their own safety and possibly hoping that if it really is the Devil's Arse he did not have a curry last night. The cavern seems to have attracted visitors from way back and in 1799 for example, the Hon. Mrs Murray of Kensington in her adventurous guide book, and try beating this for a title; *A Companion and Useful Guide to the Beauties of Scotland to the Lakes of Westmoreland, Cumberland and Lancashire; and to the Curiosities in The District of Craven, in the West Riding of Yorkshire, to which is added, a more particular Description of Scotland especially that part of it called The Highlands: by The Hon. Mrs Murray, of Kensington,* (Phew!) suggested the following requisites. 'In preparation for entering Peak Cavern one should take spare petticoats, a night cap and a yard of course flannel to prevent the discomfort of drips down ones neck. Some snuff and tobacco for the old, 'witch-looking beings' which in fact were the rope makers 'and beware of singeing your guide's beard (with a candle) when being piggy-backed across the stream'. She also added 'that anyone in possession of a long nose is at great risk from projecting rock' so not a place for Gerard Depardieu or Pinnochio to visit. All of this has long disappeared along with 'The Douglas Museum, A House of wonders' which I remember as a child somewhere along the roadway to the entrance of the cavern. Here could be seen, and

I quote from an original handbill 'a unique collection from all parts of the world. The finest collection of Cavern Formations. A collection of Locks from 4,000 years ago. The Smallest Electric Motor that will stand under a small thimble. A tiny greenhouse complete with plant-pots and flowers in bloom no bigger than your thumbnail. Handwriting that will pass through the eye of a needle' and just when you thought you could not take anymore, there was 'A Wonder in Carving. A Pair of Tongs carved from an Ordinary Match which when closed will fit inside another hollowed out to receive it. The chief point of interest in the Tongs is that they have been carved from One Solid Match and not made in Two Pieces.' All these enthralling objects along with many others were guaranteed to 'occasion wonder in the most disinterested person.' On the other hand the mind-boggling collection might just promote the thought 'Why would you want to?' Also while you were in the area, just up the road was 'The World Famous Blue-John Caverns. Now Magnificently Transformed by the Installation of Modern Electric Floodlighting' and visited by such distinguished people as 'Lord Roberts, H.G.Wells and Sir A. Conan Doyle' to name but a few. Anyway, Herbert Marrison finally spliced his last rope and died some years later. His ashes have been interred inside the cavern overlooking the rope works where he spent so much of his life. A fitting finale to a man whose hardiness and skills I greatly admired. We all shuffled back through the snow and the failing light to the car when our tutor decided he wanted visit a pub in Youlgreave.

Here I was going to write a quirky piece about how the three of us ended up in a pub in Youlgreave. Our tutor had heard there was a display of goods that had presumably been purchased by the licensee of the pub and which had formerly belonged to the Great Train Robbers while they were holed up in a Buckinghamshire farmhouse. I vaguely recall sleeping bags and cooking utensils hanging about the walls of the pub, all of which were amazingly uninteresting. Now despite an advertisement being placed by me in a newspaper local to Youlgreave and the surrounding area requesting information on this matter, no one to date has replied. From this I am forced to conclude that one of three things has occurred. Firstly, that anybody else who witnessed this display in the pub has passed on. Secondly, it never happened and I dreamt it all through a haze of alcohol, or thirdly, I had unwittingly been abducted by aliens and was in fact having a drink in a pub on another planet in a parallel universe. I feel I am very much on my own regarding this episode as sadly my student companion Kate fell victim to cancer many years ago while still young, and in all likelihood the tutor may very well be in the sort of state where he barely remembers he is the owner of the face he sees in a mirror. For the time being the whole thing remains a bit of a mystery, unless, of course, you know otherwise!

Kate and I tended to team up on projects so we arranged one Sunday morning to meet as we had been told to cover a ploughing match near to where she lived. This did not fill us with excitement but we thought we had better go all the same. On the Saturday I had caught the bus to Buxton to meet a friend who had a cave to show me that he had come across and then catch another bus to Ashbourne that afternoon and on to the cottage where Kate lived. Well one thing led to another that led to the pub that led to me missing the last bus to Ashbourne. Bravely, or stupidly I set off on foot hoping to get a lift for it is a very long and very bleak road that winds across the tops to Ashbourne. Within minutes a car pulled up alongside me and I got my first lift, but only a couple of miles up the road to Brierlow. Back on Shank's pony I continued to walk, and walk, and walk as traffic appeared to be non-existent and to cap it all it began to drizzle. I tramped on past familiar landmarks, well just two pubs, because there is little else scattered along that road and on your own as I was, trudging along in the dark can be a particularly lonely experience. By the time the Jug and Glass came into sight, a beacon of light in the mist and drizzle I was weary and desperate. I flung open the bar door and shouted above the noise of the customers, "Is anyone going Ashbourne way, I desperately need a lift?" Well, you could have heard a pin drop as it suddenly went very quiet. It was like a scene from a Clint Eastwood film where he throws open the saloon doors and everyone turns to look at him in fear. I created a similar reaction only fear was not in their eyes. I could plainly see they were thinking 'who is this bedraggled, soggy person who looks quite mad? Who in their right mind would want to share a car with him? He could be a murderer? Yes! He looks like a murderer. Are his clothes wet with rain or perhaps blood?' I stood there panting with fatigue as everyone continued to stare at me. Eventually, I blurted out "So nobody's going anywhere down the road?" The silence was finally broken as a few muttered and mumbled "No, not tonight" whereupon they turned their backs to me and carried on talking as if nothing had happened and I was not there. I went back outside into the cold, black, damp night wondering if I had handled that situation rather badly and perhaps I should go back inside and try another approach. Hopelessness kicked in for having had the sort of reception you would expect from just announcing to a bar filled with drinkers that you had the Black Death, I thought better of it and continued my lonely marathon. I tramped on as a wind whipped across the top of limestone walls barely visible in the blackness of the night. I passed Newhaven and still no traffic and by now it was eleven thirty so not much chance of it improving. The road just went on, and on, and on, as I kept going on, and on, and on, until I reached the turn-off for Tissington when I heard the sound of an approaching car. I considered throwing myself under it then at least I could put an end to this awful night, but fortunately I did not have to make the decision as the car stopped and a window was wound down releasing a cloud of cigarette smoke and beer fumes. When the fug cleared I could see a middle-aged woman in the passenger seat in a slightly dishevelled state who asked "Want a lift love? You can get in the back." The cheery sounding driver said something but slurred his words so badly I had no idea what he was saying. I gratefully climbed into the back seat. The woman, who was very much 'mutton dressed as lamb' had a short skirt revealing most of her thighs and a blouse that was more open than buttoned from which one sizeable breast seemed hell bent on escaping as she twisted around to talk to me. She was only marginally more coherent than the driver and reeked of spirits and continually made innuendos and threats to join me in the back to warm me up, although for much of the time I thought that a large wobbling breast was going to beat her to it and end up on my lap closely followed by the other large wobbling breast that was slowly putting in an appearance. She gabbled and giggled and tittered while the driver grunted, coughed and babbled in an unintelligible way, thus adding to the general mayhem as he swerved first from one side of the road, then the other, then drove down the middle yet still managed to clip the verge as we swept at break-neck speed around a corner. This threw the woman around on her seat causing her to shriek and her skirt to now rise well above her knickers as she lolloped out of control along with her out of control breasts which had almost broken free; and still he drove like a maniac with only one headlamp working peering through a windscreen partly covered in breathy condensation the rest in a fog of cigarette smoke. We continued to career along the road, swerving all over the place, the woman by now in a near state of undress as she was continually being thrown about in her seat while I hung onto whatever I could find to hang onto which at one stage was almost the woman's right breast as it lunged towards me between the two front seats like a lifebelt being thrown to a drowning man! They were both the Devil incarnate and I was on a drive to Hell! If only I'd known! I might just have preferred to carry on walking. Somehow I escaped death and got out of the car in Ashbourne with her shouting out of the window "Sure we can't take you any farther love?" before racing off at great speed around a corner and out of sight. I have no idea what time of the morning it was so I rang Kate to see if she would collect me as she still lived some miles away. The night finished with me sitting behind Kate, with no crash helmet on my head as her ancient moped displaying 'L' plates groaned and spluttered along the lanes to her cottage. Having walked the best part of sixteen miles in a few hours I was quite exhausted and as a result we missed the ploughing contest (boring anyway) and stayed in bed instead.

Sacrificing the Wife

Some of the photographic projects required more than a degree of both thought and effort and the display boards for my diploma exhibition needed filling. My next theme had to be representative of a trade or industry so I took myself off to a stonemason's yard, or to be more precise a maker of headstones. The yard was on Normanton Road, so not too far from home and by way of a change neither was it snowing. The idea for the visit came to me because my uncle Alfred had been a coffin maker for the Co-operative Society. He once told me that the small tooth on the topside of a saw near the end was for clearing out sawdust from between joints. My uncle was also an accomplished saxophonist and met his wife who was a flapper girl at one of his dance band evenings. When I think about it, the combination of being a coffin maker and a saxophone player could have proved useful for anyone wanting a creole-style funeral. He was also very good at marquetry and could have turned this into a profitable hobby by offering to inlay coffin lids with 'fleur de lis' motifs or perhaps something more demanding like a rosewood version of the Bayeux tapestry, the Rape of the Sabine Women or a pint of Guinness in ebony and hornbeam. When my uncle died, in all likelihood his funeral was arranged through the Co-Op, which begs the question did my aunt, his wife, get her Co-Op 'dividend' on the funeral expenses. This would have been considerably more than she would receive on her weekly groceries bill. Anyway, back in the stonemason's yard I clicked away at headstones in varying stages of completion, watched in wonder at a worker chiselling out an epitaph, and another hammering lead into the grooves to produce a leaded lamentation in a carved floral gravestone. Inside a workshop covered in stone dust and draped in dusty cobwebs a huge menacing saw in a cloud of spray slowly cut its way through white Italian marble, Norwegian granite and Welsh slate, but obviously not all at the same time. I took a lot of good pictures and left the works wondering what it must be like to have to work in an environment that reminded you daily of the final day, the end of the line, the point of no return. Similar, I imagine to working in an undertakers.

My grandfather took an interest in my project and invited me to where he worked in Alvaston at a place always referred to as BOBCo's which stood for the British Organ Blowing Company that could, unfortunately, be misinterpreted and translated as a smutty innuendo. In actual fact they produced motors and components for blowing air into the pipes of church organs. My grandfather was well respected because of his inventiveness and versatile manual dexterity and consequently the company was loath to let him retire even though he was well past his sell-by date. He often spoke of the times he had to creep about in underground crypts and vaults fixing electric cables and junction boxes to the sides of tombs as unintended irreverence and general lack of space went hand in hand. On one occasion he was working late in a church and the verger had forgotten he was there and locked him in. He was only released when his van was spotted later that night parked in a side lane. I do not think he was overly keen on spending a night in a cold, dark sepulchre filled with the bones of the dead, especially as both his flask of tea and sandwich box were empty which would have left him with just a few old bones to gnaw on. Unfortunately the shots I took at BOBCo's of showers of sparks from welding and angle grinding did not really inspire me, so I needed to look elsewhere, and elsewhere was the mysterious and questionable world of witchcraft and the occult.

I have to admit that my interest in the occult was initially fired-up after I had read a couple of Dennis Wheatley novels, *The Devil Rides Out* and *To the Devil a Daughter* after which I delved into the black arts with gusto. First I borrowed two massive books from Derby library, *The Book of the Dead* and the *Book of Whispering* translated from Egyptian hieroglyphics. It has to be said they did not make riveting reading, the story line was rubbish, and what with so-and-so, who begat the son of so-and-so, who then begat the son of so-and-so, it had almost as many names as the London telephone directory and who in their right mind would want to read that?! I then moved on to a far more interesting book by Alex Sanders (real name Carter, an unfortunate coincidence unless my father has taken a well-kept secret to the grave) a Lancashire lad who was the self-proclaimed King of the Witches. This came about one afternoon when his mother sent him round to grannies for his tea where he got more than he bargained for. Instead of walking into the house expecting some jam sandwiches, an Eccles cake and a beaker of Lemonade, all he got when he walked through the door was a front seat view of granny leaping about in the buff and before he knew what had hit him he quickly found himself also in the buff leaping about alongside granny. From then on it went from bad to worse and young Alex found he was doing things with granny that made him completely forget about his jam sandwiches and Eccles cake which I personally think would have been a better option than granny's idea of tea. Little wonder he turned out the way he did for the rest of his life. You can see now just how dedicated I had become to the subject and I was determined to leave no stone unturned in my voracious quest for knowledge to make my final project the best.

No such research would be complete without mentioning Aleister Crowley the self-appointed Great Beast 666 as he liked to call himself. Try getting away with writing that on the top on your exam paper or an income tax form. Despite living a drug-fuelled life that involved cavorting about with any number of naked women, in the end it did not do him much good. Why do so-called witchcraft ceremonies always require everyone to be starkers? I mean who would want to be leaping about in the middle of winter naked unless the central heating was turned up full which then makes it an expensive pastime. The pictures I found of him looked as if he had never, in his entire life heard a really funny joke and that every day was a Monday morning. Miserable or what? The final book I ploughed through was *Malus Maleficarus*, a book written in 1486 (so obviously not out in paperback) which was packed with handy, helpful tips on how to discover whether or not your next door neighbour was a witch. Say, for example your neighbour was Martha Grumpit, who lived alone, had a hairy wart on the end of her nose, kept a cat and fed it Whiskas. That could be sufficient evidence for her to find Mathew Hopkins (self-styled witch finder general and a great believer in home entertainment) banging on her door one day, and you could bet he had not come to sell her some double glazing or invite her to a Tupperware party. This being the case then Martha Grumpit would quickly have to cancel her milk and paper deliveries because she would be accused of being in league with the devil, a wart being enough to condemn her (they were not too fussy about proof in the Middle Ages) and that would be the end of her. *Malus Maleficarus* then gave instructions on how to entertain a village of bored peasants on a Saturday afternoon. A public hanging always went down well, but even more popular was a bit of witch burning. While poor old Martha Grumpit was having a jolly good roasting, she would unwittingly be providing an excuse for a village get-together involving some communal jeering while keeping warm around the fire with the kids toasting a few marshmallows on a stick and the promise of baked potatoes later. It brought the whole village together the likes of which you rarely witness these days. What with constant cut-backs on council funds, the ever rising price of kindling wood and the car parking difficulties that would be created by a witch burning, nobody bothers anymore and so another ancient tradition is lost forever. Next thing you know there will be a ban on cheese-rolling.

Meanwhile back on the college campus my devotion to my project had caught the attention of one of the porters who announced to me one morning that he might possibly be able to get me some genuine occult props for my photographs. This sounded promising and a week later, as good as his word, he presented me with a pair of daggers allegedly used by a local coven for sacrificial ceremonies. Whether or not they had been used to dispatch some young nubile wench or someone's pet gerbil on an altar to 'Old Nick' will never be known, but a couple of weeks later he asked for them back as 'they' from the coven were after him presumably for nicking them in the first place. I refused to hand them over and after a period of time he became rather withdrawn, so I can only speculate on whether 'they' later sacrificed him on someone's kitchen table or perhaps made him have sex with a goat. The outcome will remain a mystery for I left college shortly afterwards and never saw him again. However, after all this exhaustive research I was ready for the 'big shoot' having persuaded my wife Carol (Okay, Okay, I will wash the dinner pots for a week) to be sacrificed in the back bedroom.

I had some previous experience of painting on walls so producing a huge pentagram in black paint surrounded by cabalistic symbols whose meanings were lost on me and for all I know could have said 'Two extra pints please, the money's under the doormat' was not too much of a challenge. Wall painting was a trait I had inherited from my artistic mother who would paint on the walls of the family home and once created a woodland scene with a pathway, which had it been for real would have led through the wall and inconveniently into the back of next doors piano. She also painted a lake scene on a wall the other side of which was the lavatory and I had calculated that again, had this been the real thing then sitting in the privy meant that only my head would have been above water which would have been slightly awkward coupled with a bit of a swim to the shoreline, the only dry place to keep the toilet roll. Well your thoughts tend to wander all over the place when you are sat on the loo killing time. Following in the tradition of mother's murals I was once asked to paint a large alpine scene on the living room wall of a friend's house which I completed over several weekends. Imagine my chagrin when I discovered a year later that they had painted over it in order to sell their house. Michelangelo, I am sure would have sympathised with me had he looked up one day to find that some half-witted council official had ordered the Sistine Chapel ceiling to be painted over in 'a hint of apple' emulsion! As pentagrams go, mine looked pretty good, so with some spooky green lighting, two black candles with coffin nails stuck through them the scene was set. Carol was laid out on a table altar loosely wrapped in a piece of flimsy curtain netting as she refused point blank to pose in the nude and have all my college mates leering at her during my diploma display. I was poised over her with my newly acquired sacrificial dagger about to plunge it into her chest. Though I say it myself the picture was first class even though I did not go through with the complete ritual as we ran out of time because Carol had to get the dinner underway. Unbeknown to me it seems my mother had got wind of my occult shenanigans and was most concerned about my intentions, and my sanity, and my ritualistic attempt to slaughter my own wife. Well, I must say I did not think it was that much out of the ordinary considering my mother had married a man who in his youth had become a member of the British Union of Fascists, or Oswald Mosley's 'brown shirts' as they were more commonly known and had held a secret meeting in the cellar of my granny's house. In truth it was only a very short-lived secret meeting for granny soon discovered them, boxed them all around the ears and threw them out into the street. Granny was a force to be reckoned with and if only she had been sent to Berlin during the war, she would have soon located Hitler's secret bunker, marched in and boxed his ears good and proper as well! Other photographs to accompany the project which was meant to be a mock-up of a feature article in a weekend supplement included an eerily lit gravestone filched from a cemetery that had become completely overgrown, neglected and badly vandalised with most of the graves broken open and headstones smashed. During the latter part of the Sixties Derby was being torn apart by planners and bulldozers and many fine buildings were reduced to rubble including churches and graveyards. Consequently I do not feel too guilty about a clandestine trip one dark night riding pillion on a friend's scooter with a headstone tucked under my arm. I can also recall a lad on my course arriving at college one day and photographing a skull in one of the studios which did not go down too well with the tutors, for they were well aware of where it had come from and as far as they were concerned this was tantamount to grave robbing which really is a crime.

The trouble with being at college on a photographic course is people are for ever asking you to take pictures for them in the hopes that they will get good photographs at a rock-bottom price. They work on the premise that because you are a student and naturally hard-up anything is better than nothing. I remember having to rush over to Heanor one morning because Carol's mother thought that old Randy was about to go to that big kennel up in the sky and wanted me to photograph him before he went. When I arrived, Randy did indeed look as though he was about to throw in the towel, so it was with some considerable effort that we managed to coax him out onto the front doorstep and into the sunshine for his last portrait.

We tried to prop him up so he did not look like he had already passed on, but he was having none of it and just wanted to flop down on the pathway as if resigned to his fate. Carol's mother persisted for a while and at one point I was wondering if she wanted old Randy to raise a smile at the same time, or maybe wave a paw joyously at the camera, but he was past all this, so I took the picture where he lay. Later that day, Randy cashed in his chips and left for that doggy Valhalla where 'walkies' are heavenly and meaty marrow bones plentiful. The photograph became a treasured keepsake despite Randy appearing to be already dead in the picture, but I suppose at the end of the day and to use modern parlance, he just 'couldn't be arsed!'

Next up was my granny and grandpa's Golden Wedding Anniversary, and what a sorry saga that turned out to be. It was held in Allestree and members of the family from far and wide flocked to this grand occasion to talk themselves hoarse in a non-stop babble of 'I can't remember when I saw you last? Was it at Florry's funeral, or when their Marj' got married?' and 'Well, haven't you grown since I last saw you, and you're at university now are you? You always were a bookworm wasn't she Len? I say she was always a bookworm, just like your father. He always had his head stuck in a book. Sometimes you couldn't get him out of the lavatory for hours, could you Len. I say you couldn't... oh never mind'; and all served up with gallons of tea, a few lagers and some glasses of sherry. How they managed to shut up long enough to stuff a ham sandwich or a sausage roll into their mouths will remain a secret art peculiar to the elderly. I moved among the continual bedlam taking pictures of relatives and the obligatory group gatherings so everyone was covered and they could all have photographs of this momentous occasion, or so they thought. Monday morning saw me in the college darkroom contemplating suicide and trying to decide whether drowning in the tank of developer would be preferable to drowning in the tank of fixer. On the side bench lay my camera with the back open and a length of film hanging out taunting me with its two rows of torn sprocket holes; a film that had never gone through the camera because it had somehow become jammed and ripped from the very start and as a result I had about fifty pictures all taken on the same frame. I epitomised complete incompetence, and granny was going to kill me, or at the very least cross me off her will. I was distraught. I was doomed. I was in serious trouble. Understandably, granny was more than a bit vexed and gave me quite a dressing down, because that occasion was never going to be repeated and I had nothing to show for it apart from a red face and ringing ears. Reportage photography was never my forte as my sister will readily testify after she laboured under the illusion that I would produce a fine collection of photographic memories of her 'big day' which as it turned out photographically, was an illusion. I pranced about with my camera and Weston Master exposure meter calculating the light and snapping away as if there was no tomorrow, which would have been a blessing for me because tomorrow revealed an overexposed film resulting in a collection of faint, ethereal looking pictures. My sister really should have known better then to trust me with the task. It did cross my mind that like many people she might eventually get divorced and I could be more successful a second time around, but she is still married to the same man to this day. Well! That is sisters for you, anything to be awkward!

However, I did not just reserve carelessness for important occasions only for I managed it on the home front just as easily. I sometimes found it necessary to unload and reload roll and sheet films at home if I was busy with a project and required lots of film, so I used the cupboard under the stairs as a dark room. It was far from ideal if only for the simple fact that the light switch inside was broken and had bare terminals exposed so each time I switched it on in the dark, something I tried to avoid as much as possible, I normally electrocuted myself. This would hit me as an intense zinging pain that shot through my fingers closely followed by an aching throbbing arm. I am not too sure about the therapeutic qualities or benefits of self-electrification, if indeed there are any, but it certainly gives you that 'wide awake' sensation but not sufficient to stop me getting electrocuted many times, or more importantly make an effort to repair the switch. Electricity and I have had many close encounters in the past. Take, for example, the time I was in a rush to attend a party and my tape recorder was needed to provide the music. Because it sat on a shelf at home with the cable running through a hole in the shelf I decided I could not be bothered to take off the plug, so after unplugging the machine from an adaptor I cut through the cable with a pair of scissors. I reckon now that ninety-nine people out of a hundred could easily write the next line and get it right. Yes, it was the wrong plug I took out of the adaptor and yes, there was a flash as an electric shock seared through my arm after first welding together the blades of the scissors. Perhaps the worst incident was when I did not actually get a shock, strange though that may sound. I was rewiring a pair of alcove lights and had switched off at the wall before taking off the old fittings. As I did not have a cable stripper I cut around the plastic covering the wire with a metal craft blade and pulled off the surplus with my teeth. Imagine my surprise when everything was back in place and I came to place a light bulb into the new socket and the thing lit up in my hand. Somehow the switch had not gone off properly and consequently the wires had been live throughout the entire procedure! It makes my toes curl whenever I think about those live wires in my mouth. Theoretically they should either have killed me, or failing that, blown all of my teeth out cleared my sinuses and scorched the collar of my shirt. I could have spent the rest of my life half-baked, gormless and gummy. Suddenly an image of Jumbo springs to mind.

Anyway, back to the cupboard under the stairs. A neighbour knocked on the door one evening asking if I could unload his camera for him in my dark cupboard as the film had become jammed and he did not want to ruin the film; and while I was at it could I process it and run some prints off for him. The thing is I did not really know him that well, and his wife I did not know at all until I printed from the negatives of his film. It was an unexpected revelation to discover that I was printing pictures of her completely naked with only a fine crop of hair covering (more or less) her modesty as she cavorted about their bedroom. You will understand when I say that I felt I knew her a little better after seeing the prints even though I had still not met her for real. When I handed them over to the neighbour he never said a word about the contents merely asking me what I thought about them as pictures. Resisting the obvious comment about overexposure I simply said that he needed some better lighting. He then asked me if I had the time whether I could show him what I meant, implying that his wife would be in the nip and quite possibly all three of us would end up in the nip. Now I am not suggesting that his young wife was unattractive, but she did have short frizzy red hair (at both ends as it turned out) a bony body with marble-white skin and the word necrophilia kept floating through my mind. Her husband, the instigator of all this looked uncannily like Woody Allen and was perhaps as neurotic, so I reckoned that as a 'menage a trois' it was not looking too promising, so consequently I never did find the time and he never asked again. On reflection I suppose it would have been more visually rewarding and socially more memorable than having to photograph a moribund Randy in the front garden.

Regardless of the fact that my track record as a budding photographer was not looking too good I did present a pretty reasonable diploma display and as predicted, I got away with my mini thesis on Cave Photography knowing it was a field that none of my tutors had ever undertaken and consequently inhibited their criticism. The end result was that I got my Diploma in Creative Photography which I could proudly carry throughout the rest of my life safe in the knowledge that some block-head in administration had, after my three years of study manage to misspell my name. All I had to do now was find a job as a photographer. It seemed that getting any chance of work would mean leaving Derby which I was prepared to do, although that would not be easy for I had spent my childhood and youth in the Peak District and all my relatives lived in and around Derby. Would they all miss my visits I wondered? They had all been a great part of my life and so were the memories and experiences with which I associated a kind of stability. Their stories and their tales would follow me through life. In short, they were my history.

The Four Georges

Take my father for example. He had always done the same job at the same place for as long as I can remember and hated almost every day spent there, but his work ethic meant he was loyal to his boss and despite fairly constant ill health he rarely missed a day right up to his golden handshake. He worked for a horticultural implements firm called The Standard Manufacturing Company, a truly inspirational name that would make any employee leap out of bed in the morning eager to get to work. It was housed by Rowditch Park in an aged, gloomy ex-army barracks whose dusty cob-webbed, white distempered interior resembled a cross between a prison and a Dickensian sweatshop. Here my father made, as a handbill proudly announces; 'Standard' tree pruning implements, all sizes from 3 feet to 30 feet, also Secateurs, Pole saws, Fruit pickers, Rotary hoes and 'Leaf-lifters' their long handled fruit pickers being particularly popular overseas, especially Africa. This is merely a passing thought, but African traders could have saved themselves considerable expense if they had taken the initiative to train a giraffe with a net bag slung beneath its chin to gather coconuts and bunches of bananas. As I say, it was merely a passing thought.

Inside the depressing building were heavy antique metal presses and a paint shop that reeked of lung gasping cellulose paint which did my father's one remaining lung no good at all when he was on paint spraying duty. This experience was probably the reason why he avoided anything to do with paint at home. Only once do I recall him very reluctantly painting the living room ceiling with distemper which was a particularly messy business. Anything that could be moved was moved out of the room or covered over to protect it from the watery, sloppy paint. Even the windows were covered over with distemper to stop people looking in and once dry it was ideal for my sister and me to scrape away at it drawing funny faces with our finger nails. Back then people were very conscious about others looking in from outside which could well have been a left-over from when streets of terraced houses faced right onto the pavement and it was easy to peer in through the window. Old habits die hard. Curtains were always drawn at the onset of twilight and net curtains had the same effect during the day. This was particularly important in the past when the tradition still existed of having a deceased family member laid out in a coffin in the front parlour for anyone to come in and pay their last respects. On these occasions curtains remained drawn all day for it was considered highly disrespectful to peer in through the window, whereas relatives, neighbours and friends of the deceased were welcome to come and gaze at the corpse.

"Hello Lil, didn't expect to see you here" said Nora, surprised to see her neighbour from three doors down in the parlour. "I thought you and uncle Stanley here never got on?"

"Well, we didn't always see eye to eye that's for sure, what with his damned pigeons forever pooing on my washing" replied Lil with her arms folded firmly across her matronly chest. "But for all that" she continued, "he wasn't such a bad old stick."

"Ah well, let bygones be bygones eh" answered Nora balancing a glass of sherry on the edge of uncle Stanley's coffin. "Eighty-seven last week" Nora continued. "Ya can't say he didn't have a good innings." (Why is a person's life-span always likened to a cricket match?)

"I saw him only last Friday in the Roebuck" started Lil, "having his usual couple of pints of IPA. I thought to me sel' then he were lookin' a bit peaky. Ya know, a bit sorta grey int' face. I said to our Bert when I got home, I said that Stanley'll not be too long for this world, an' here he is gone."

"Well I never, and what did your Bert say?" asked Nora, draining the last of the sherry from her glass.

"Now't much as usual. You know our Bert, once he's got his face glued t' telly watchin' football, well, he would'na notice if the ruddy Russians had invaded our house. Daft beggar that he is. T' be 'onest' Lil rambled on, "I reckon Stanleys lookin' better now than he were int' pub last week."

"Ya might be right there" agreed Nora "He looks quite well just now, an' in his best suit as well. Bless. Fancy a sherry our Lil?"

"Don't mind if I do." And so the pair of them wandered out of the parlour leaving uncle Stanley in his box as they headed for the bottle of sherry on the living room sideboard. Now days if you see a house with the curtains drawn all day, then it is probably occupied by students recovering from the previous night's drug-fuelled, booze-sodden orgy and still in their beds in a comatose state. Anyway, back to the distempering of the living room ceiling. After several hours of banging and slapping and cursing my father would emerge from the room in his trademark brown works coat and a beret crammed on his head (he thought this gave him a savoir faire French artist look) both of which were liberally covered with enough white paint to make him appear as if an entire colony of sea gannets had dropped a year's worth of guano over him. Normally people associate the word distemper with the highly infectious disease of dogs which gives them a fever and a bad cough. My father managed to look as if he had caught distemper during his painting antics for his face was fever red and he coughed a lot anyway. Everyone wore drab brown coats where he worked and rarely got outside except to load pruners onto the back of a waiting flat-bed lorry. Probably the only bonus of working there was that the building was situated within a high brick wall enclave the majority of which was grassed over for use as a tennis court and on a tea break a gaggle of leering brown coated lechers would sit back and enjoy the sight of bare thighs and bouncing breasts as a couple of young ladies played out a game of tennis. Unfortunately those days are long gone and the barracks are now boarded over with smashed windows and weeds growing from the walls, while the grass tennis courts remain uncut and neglected, as indeed do the row of cottages that also overlooked this sheltered green patch that once had a certain charm about it on a warm summer afternoon.

Although it was only a small company it did manage in 1947 a works outing to Skegness and there is a photograph showing everyone dressed in suits, pullovers, shirts and ties along with some of the office ladies well wrapped up in belted overcoats looking as if the weather had proved to be rather more inclement than they had expected. They probably enjoyed the outing for the most part, although a number of bemused faces would seem to suggest that perhaps the tide was out and not their idea of the seaside! A picture of them at an annual Christmas dinner is even worse. It was possibly held in the Rowditch tennis pavilion and looks not unlike the last meal of the condemned, for not one person sitting around the table in the photograph I have is smiling. But then, looking at the meagre spread of a few sandwiches, biscuits, mince pies and small fancy cakes it is little wonder they are a tad underwhelmed for a cornucopia of festive food it is not; and with only two bottles of red wine between eleven men it looks as bleak as the painted brick interior of the building where it is being held.

During the early war years my father signed up as a Special Constable and wore a tin hat with the word 'POLICE' emblazoned across the front. Once when he was on night duty in the town he heard giggling sounds coming from within the dark interior of an air-raid shelter so he switched on his torch and peered into the entrance. In his best official policeman's voice he shouted 'What's going on here then? Come on let's be havin' you' to which a very gruff and menacing sounding voice replied, 'Put that f…..g light out and f..k off mate.' Now my father was not by nature an aggressive man and sensing more than a degree of intimidation and in the interests of self-preservation, he did just that! He reckoned it would have been some service chap doing his duty on the home front of a willing wench who was offering up her homely front as her contribution to the war effort. He also joined the Home Guard as his ill health rendered him unfit for overseas service and at the finish of the war all he had to show for his efforts was the Defence medal (Kings Commendation for brave conduct, Civil) and a khaki Great coat which over the years a few hungry moths managed to destroy what the Luftwaffe had failed to do. His main contribution during those dark years was to train as an Aero Engine Fitter and eventually be let loose on repairing the damaged planes that came in to RAF Cosford during which time he managed to damage one himself. He was at the controls (steering) of a Spitfire that was being towed under cover when it passed too close to a tree and he took the wing tip off. Naturally, he never owned up to this mishap, but some time later divine justice played its hand in the shape of a Blenheim bomber that unexpectedly rolled backwards down a runway and went over his foot. However, life at times could be quite idyllic and during those long, hot summers of the early forties, my father spent much of his time painting trees with green paint (don't ask) or picking blackberries and getting a good tan. Back on the home front my mother, whose talents once extended to artistically decorating porcelain for Crown Derby china now stayed at home getting pregnant and knitting babywear for my sister who would shortly be putting in an appearance and being fashion conscience from the start would be demanding the latest in babywear. 'Oh, really mother, I can't possibly wear those knitted bootees, they really smack of wartime austerity. I mean, look around you, simply every baby is wearing them. I can't be seen out in my pram in those now can I?' Being a proficient dressmaker my mother continually kitted both herself and my sister out in frocks and blouses and skirts right up until my sister got married and left home. My mother feeling socially isolated then took a job in a tiny kiosk (not big enough inside to swing a cat round, not that she ever tried) jammed in the corner of a shop entrance just down from the Spot. The Spot in those days was notorious for its underground toilets and nefarious activities and my mother spent her days within whiffing distance as she served her many regulars with cigarettes and chocolate bars.

The thing about leaving Derby and all my relatives was that there were so many of them and I was only just about making sense of who was related to whom and my relationship to them. For a start my father was called George and I had three uncles who were also called George, so you can appreciate just how confusing that could become during a conversation. In truth one was a great uncle, but I rarely saw him. He was a big, burly and ungainly man and my first memory of him as a youngster was being trapped in the back of my grandfather's van going to a family party. Great uncle George had already downed a few beers and was lolloping about and flapping his arms singing something about 'and down came a ruddy great blackbird and pecked off her nose. Squawk, squawk!' as he sprayed my sister and I in beery saliva. He continued to crash around the back of the van and the image of that black, unkempt, maniacally grinning man pretending to be a blackbird hell bent on nasal annihilation was a mesmerising and nightmarish experience that has stayed with me to this day. He really was the bogey man. He was married to my aunt Rosie, her of the Hepatitis pinafore, which was an apt name (Rosie that is, not Hepatitis) as she always had ruddy cheeks and between them (my uncle and aunt that is, not her cheeks) they adopted a boy and a girl as aunt Rosie's mother, my great grandma said they could only get married provided they did not make children as aunt Rosie was 'too weak to bear children.' Yet when I consider the conditions they lived in I think robust would have been a more suitable description. The house was never clean and they kept coal in a bath downstairs and strangely, aunt Rosie smiled through it all, in fact she seemed to smile through everything all of the time as if the smile was a permanent fixture, but whether it was a smile of happiness, or the smile of someone mildly mad might be difficult to determine. I recall how she even smiled at my father's funeral and brought along a camera to take pictures of the occasion. I am not sure what prompted this gesture because nobody else was smiling that day, least of all my father. Looking on the bright side at least she refrained from taking any shots actually inside the crematorium, or later nipping down to the undertaker in Macklin Street and taking a 'macro' view inside my father's urn. There would have been plenty of opportunity for this to happen as the urn sat on a shelf for the best part of six months until I collected it. I think by then they were really getting cheesed off with having to keep dusting the thing and were glad to see the back of it. I finally scattered my father's ashes somewhat clumsily into the wind at Black Rocks because of his great love for the Peak District. I would like my own ashes when the time comes thrown into the river Wye at Water-cum-Jolly Dale so I can float through glorious Monsal Dale and on past Ashford in the Water, provided of course, the brown trout do not mistake my ashes for someone emptying a large tub of Tetrafin goldfish food into the water and I get eaten before I have even started my journey!

Great uncle George had in the past fancied himself as a bit of a horticulturist and had taken to growing tomatoes in the front bedroom window, which would have been fine except for his over enthusiastic watering that cascaded daily through the ceiling and down the walls of the parlour. Luckily at this stage my great granny had yet to occupy the downstairs front room as her bedroom or she might very well have puzzled over her apparent daily incontinence. Great uncle George seemed oblivious to such consequences and during his days of owning an allotment off Kedleston Road he was busily working out how to get water to his patch from a standpipe some distance away. He came up with a simple and effective plan having realised that the mains pipe bordered his plot which meant his problems would be solved by thrusting his spade through the mains, which he did and water immediately sprayed over his plot. So far, so good, but what he had not fathomed out was how to turn off the water which continued to spray over his plot and started to flood all the other plots as the entire allotment slowly disappeared under the deluge of water. Eventually a flood covered the whole area and I am talking here of a flood of biblical proportions that would have sent Noah fleeing to the nearest hilltop and start frantically bashing nails into planks of wood and gathering up the neighbourhood cats, dogs and budgerigars in pairs. By now it had dawned on great uncle George that there had been a noticeable flaw in his plan, so he took the only sensible option open to him which was to run away and hide in the outside lavatory at home where he was discovered later by a couple of not very jolly policemen. They were none too pleased about his antics and neither were the other allotment holders as they gazed out over the expanse of water covering their prize vegetables, particularly as not one of them had intended growing rice that year! Great uncle George was outlived by his wife Rosie who in her dotage dressed herself completely in black and went into the business of gate-crashing funerals. This normally got her a free afternoon tea and it is unlikely that anyone would approach her and ask how she knew the deceased because she would be wearing that smile which would seem to suggest she was friendly, but which at close quarter unnerved people who consequently left her alone. This was an unfortunate side to her character because she was really a good hearted soul who always meant well, but perhaps her intentions were badly orchestrated and therefore, misinterpreted.

Another George, perhaps the most notorious of my uncles lived opposite me in Chaddesden. He used to be a cook in the navy, a fact that makes my jaw drop with disbelief as he was always looked upon as a walking health hazard and could have started the Bubonic plague at the drop of a hat. The fact that kids playing in the street outside his house often sang the old plague rhyme;

'Ring-a-ring of roses,
A pocketful of posies,
Attischo, attischo,
We all fall down.'

was probably pure coincidence, I think? Uncle George was not a great believer in washing and for the most part his bath was redundant and left to dead spiders that had been unable to climb out. His general persona was unwholesome and his fingers heavily stained with nicotine that could hardly have got much browner had he roasted them for an hour in an oven at Gas mark 6. He was a postman, an avid angler, a keen stamp collector and an outstanding example of self-neglect. He was also an ardent member of the Royal Observer Corps into which he somehow managed to rope my father. They were both kitted out in RAF style uniforms and issued with a lot of paraphernalia about methods of detecting enemy aircraft. These included charts depicting silhouettes of various aircraft to enable them to spot the difference between an incoming Wellington bomber or a Messerschmitt flying over our house, unless it was night time, in which case my father would be unable to spot anything as my mother always insisted on the curtains being closed. The two of them normally attended observation instruction once a week and as this was in the fifties it included monitoring radioactive fall-out, so if they returned home glowing and looking a little peaky then we knew they had found some. The Royal Observer Corps motto is 'Forewarned is Forearmed' which would have been useful on the home front with regard to the few instances my uncle unexpectedly called leaving on the carpet a trail of eczema scratchings from his legs along with an overpowering stench of stale Cigarillos which he smoked constantly. Such an aftermath would send my mother fleeing for the vacuum cleaner, then waving a bottle of Airwick around the house. This normally lived in the lavatory, but she would bring it out on special occasions like this and waft it about the room. Airwick at that time was quite literally a sort of felt wick stuck in a bottle of green gunk that could be pulled up a bit at a time to release an aroma that was difficult to associate with anything else but a lavatory. The days of Pine, Lavender and Sea Breeze aerosol spray cans was yet to come. It was on occasions like this that my father realised the short comings of the Royal Observer Corps by not issuing a chart showing the silhouette my uncle George targeting the gate of our front garden.

Uncle George was a first class example of the complete opposite of a fashionista. He presented himself badly and was rarely seen wearing anything else except his dishevelled Post Office uniform. The words, fashion, smart, ironed and clean did not exist in his vocabulary. Although there is no doubt in my mind that my uncle George was fairly knowledgeable on a miscellany of topics he unfortunately laboured under the illusion that he knew everything about everything which tended to get right up folk's nasal passages. He had an extremely exasperating habit of ending his theories, his hypothesises and his opinions by looking you straight in the eyes, raising his eyebrows a little and with a slight smirk on his face announce, 'I think you'll find I'm right.' Now nobody likes a know-all and many times throughout his life my uncle must have found himself, though not necessarily aware of it, very close to death as the person he was in conversation with stoically fought back a desire to kill him on the spot. When I got my first Landrover for example, he sauntered across the road one day and in that knowing manner of his announced that if I should ever find myself with a leaking radiator then it could be cured by putting oats in with the water. He stood looking at me with that, by now, famous 'fountain of knowledge' expression on his face as I considered the prospect of an exploding radiator blocked by swollen oats, or the possibility of driving four or five miles and draining the radiator to get a bowlful of hot porridge. He outlived his long suffering wife and over the following years gradually became engulfed in his own untidiness as the kitchen where he spent much of his time disappeared beneath mountains of newspapers, journals and opened mail to the extent that there was never a spare chair to sit on without first removing heaps of rubbish. If he was not reading a paper then he would be peering through round-rimmed spectacles with bottle-bottom lenses at a six inch screen portable television, or straining to hear police conversations as he tuned into their frequency to listen to reports on burglaries, domestic crisis or a traffic accident. Quite what he gained from this activity is questionable except, of course, he would know about something before it became public knowledge, thus allowing him to boast knowingly as if he was party to some special MI5 information that had been personally conveyed to him at his secret headquarters hidden deep inside the rubbish-tip of his kitchen. Yet among all this disorder he kept a pet cockatiel that spent most of its time perched on my uncle's shoulder. As he wandered about the house like a decrepit Long John Silver the cockatiel happily defecated down the back of his already soiled and shabby ex-Post Office jacket. Uncle George seemed oblivious of this fact and would open the door to the milkman, or the rent man, or whoever might call regardless of the fact that when he turned to fetch some money it was clearly visible that the back of his jacket was heavily encrusted with enough excrement to fertilise a half acre field. Uncle George was without any doubt a 'one off' and I wondered if he would miss our occasional chats about cacti, car engines, Vesuvius, cloud formations, photography and all manner of things. I particularly mentioned the subject of photography because for probably the first and only time in his life my uncle was forced to admit that I knew more about the subject than he did because I had studied photography for three years which placed him at an obvious disadvantage. It was a much coveted moment in history and I was there!

The last George, who in fact is my only remaining uncle was about as extreme as one could get from the previous one. He and my aunt were my godparents and lived originally in a neat, tidy terraced house just up from the cemetery on Uttoxeter New Road. They owned the Alsatian dog that I used to walk to meet my spasmodic girlfriend at the Greyhound Stadium. My uncle was an ardent fan of both cricket and football neither of which has ever held any interest for me, although I will admit to there being something quintessentially English about 'leather on willow', the village cricket field, a warm summer afternoon and tea in the pavilion at half-time. However, my opinion on football is that if nobody in the entire world ever kicked a football ever again, then that would suit me just fine.

My aunt on the other hand as well as being young and glamorous had an interest in classical music, so I would sometimes lug my Grundig tape-recorder around to their house of an evening and we would listen to Grieg, Chopin, Mendelssohn and many other composers while my uncle was away at a cricket club meeting. Uncle George worked at the locomotive works off Siddals Road as a plumber fitting miles of pipework to both steam and diesel locomotives, yet his introduction to this profession began at the HMV (His Master's Voice) factory down south. At first it would seem that the connection between vinyl records and plumbing is a tenuous one until you consider that it was a sizeable factory employing a lot of people, all with bladders that would need to be taken to a lavatory now and then, hence the need for a plumber or two. He was only in his late teens and easily embarrassed by the factory girls who would tease him by sitting along the tables swinging their legs around. He found a flash of thigh very distracting for a young lad with only a hot blow lamp in his hand and a pocketful of compression joints. Apparently the girls were not even concerned if they came across my uncle above a cubicle working on a cistern as they would simply carry on, drop their knickers and get on with it (brazen hussies) being quite indifferent about revealing their plumbing system to my uncle nervously grasping a monkey wrench while fiddling to free a sticking ball-cock. I think he was better off working on locomotives. A man knows where he stands with locomotives and can be safe in the knowledge that as he concentrates on soldering a copper elbow he will not suddenly be confronted by a promiscuous young tease with her knickers round her knees.

Out of all my relatives I think my paternal granny played the biggest role in my life because she always came up with the goods. As a child she was the one that furnished me with chocolate biscuits, ice cream, fizzy pop, fish and chips and later a new bicycle. She was quite big and a 'no nonsense' kind of person with a good heart and always ready to help out in situations. There was, for instance, the elderly Mrs Ollerenshaw who lived a few doors down the street and granny would keep an eye on her for the woman was not too stable on her feet and often needed help in getting from A to B, with A being her fireside armchair, and B being the lavatory.

I vividly recall the day when granny returned from Mrs Ollerenshaw and launched into conversation with grandpa who was lying in his usual place on the settee, the cat asleep on his stomach while he watched the cricket at Edgbaston on the television.

"That poor Mrs Ollerenshaw" granny started, "I don't think she'll be long for this world, I say, I don't think she'll be long for this world. Are you listening to me Len?"

"Er, yes" muttered grandpa not taking his eyes off the screen.

"I had to take her to the lavatory and what a state she's in. I couldn't believe the state she's in. I tell you when I lifted her off the seat well, you should have seen it. You could have knocked me down with a feather. Her haemorrhoids just came away from her. You should have seen it."

"Ugh" was all grandpa had to say for he was not in the least interested in seeing Mrs Ollerenshaw's haemorrhoids or anyone else's haemorrhoids for that matter. All he wanted to see was the cricket.

"I couldn't believe it" granny continued, "Just like grapes they were, I say just like grapes. Did you hear me?"

"Yes, yes, just like grapes" retorted grandpa trying desperately to concentrate on the cricket match.

"I don't know what's to become of her. Never seen anything like it. Hanging down like grapes they were" continued granny from the kitchen where she had gone to put the kettle on. "Just like a bunch of grapes" she repeated to herself.

Now putting Mrs Ollerenshaw's haemorrhoids to one side for a moment, not that you would want to unless you were wearing rubber gloves, she had told granny that I could go through some books she was throwing out and take anything I wanted. I rushed off down the street and let myself into her front room. I was very much hoping that Mrs Ollerenshaw was not going to put in an appearance while I was there, as already my imagination after listening to granny's tale was running riot, with mental images of bloomers, buttocks and bunches of grapes being trailed across the floor in my direction in the wake of Mrs Ollerenshaw. The last thing I had in mind was for this to become a reality as I set about rapidly going through the small pile of books left out on the carpet. There was George Eliot's

Mill on the Floss, The Cloister and the Hearth by Charles Reade and H. E. Bates, *Fair stood the Wind for France* which turned out to be a truly gripping read. The most coveted book was a slightly worse for wear edition of Rev. J. G. Woods, *Popular Natural History* that was packed with amazing information and inspirational engravings of everything in the natural world, and it still graces my book cabinet to this day. There were also two volumes of *The Quiver* containing moral sermons for Sunday reading (one to miss, I fancy) which had no appeal but I took them anyway because they were old. These and a few other books formed the basis for my own personal collection which over the years grew as my passion for literature developed into a vast and eclectic library of my own.

Meanwhile, my grandpa was beginning to lose the plot of the cricket due to the saga of Mrs Ollerenshaw's haemorrhoids continually interrupting his concentration, and just when he thought it was all over he suddenly found himself bearing another onslaught of granny's tongue.

"The fires nearly out Len" she shouted to him in an accusing tone. "Are you going to get some coal up from the cellar? We need some coal on the grate."

"Right" answered grandpa, but making no effort to move from his comfortable position on the settee. Granny was becoming increasingly vexed at grandpa's inactivity so she bellowed at him from the doorway of the kitchen, words that have now become immortal and written forever in the annals of my family's history, 'LEN, THE GRATE!!' There had of course been Alexander the Great, Catherine the Great and King Alfred the Great, and yet here ranking alongside these immortal figures from history was my grandpa, exulted to the heady position of Len the Grate; a man from humble beginnings who now teetered on the very brink of canonisation to become the patron saint of coal buckets and nutty slack! It was indeed history in the making and I was there to witness the event. Reluctantly grandpa rose from the settee, went down to the cellar, fetched a bucket of coal and threw some on the grate before going back to his cricket. I thought he carried out the procedure rather too casually as it lacked both a sense of ceremony and panache, but maybe he needed to put some practice in, for being 'Len the Grate' is not something you can slip into overnight. The end result was that from that day forth my grandpa was always referred to as 'Len the Grate' a cognomen that followed him to his grave.

The thing about my grandpa was that he had had an interesting life having soldiered and survived both World Wars including the Somme and Passchendaele, and few can lay claim to that. While recovering from an injury at a training camp in France he unwittingly became responsible for initiating a mutiny in the British army, a story that remained a secret for many years. He had apparently complained to his Medical Officer about various conditions that he was expected to cope with, which he considered unfair, as he was recovering from a war wound and asked to be made exempt. The MO granted him permission to abstain from further duties and when the word got around there was a very long queue to be seen outside the MO's office. However, the MO quickly caught on to what was afoot and refused everybody else which, not surprisingly, went down like a lead balloon. The disgruntled troops rallied that evening, broke camp and marched into town shooting any officer who stood in their way and throwing them over a bridge. The rioting mob were finally rounded up and sent off the following day to the front line from which a mere handful survived to tell the tale of the mutiny. Years ago Yorkshire television made a documentary based on a book written about the event called the *Monocled Mutineer* but unfortunately my grandpa was too late to contribute to the programme. However, there was a part of the training ground called Spearmint Hill where the soldiers were shot at by conscientious objectors called 'canaries' (being yellow in the opinion of the fighting man and to be fired on by them did not sit well with the average Tommy Atkin) to make the training seem more real. Somehow this fact got back to Wrigleys who sent my grandpa a large box of chewing gum which would have been fine had it not been for the fact that by now he was very old, very frail and had very few teeth. Gumming your way through a packet of chewing gum would be a laborious, frustrating and pointless exercise. You could construe this as a kind of anachronism for the war itself.

While still on the subject of war, my grandpa had won medals for being a crack-shot and once found himself with a mate stuck in a wet, muddy shell hole in the area always known as 'no-mans-land' between enemy lines. Seemingly at a loss for something to do the mate bet my grandpa that he could not hit a crow that was sitting on the blasted, charred remains of a tree some distance away. Grandpa raised his rifle, took aim, bang went the gun and down fell the crow. Before either of them were able to pass comment, all hell broke loose as the English thought the Germans were starting an attack, and the Germans thought the English had started the attack. With bullets whizzing overhead and shells exploding everywhere, the pair of them took cover and cowered in the hole for the ten minute duration of the battle which they had started. Grandpa never spoke much about the war and life in the trenches or his POW experiences in World War Two. I guess it was not a lot of fun, although he was a natural born comedian and no doubt did his best to find the funny aspect of a dire situation whenever possible. His few pieces of war memorabilia I very much treasure and I wear the ring to this day that my grandpa swopped a chunk of bread for from a Polish prisoner who had made the silver ring with a small heart upon it. My grandpa wore it as did my father before me, and no doubt one of my own sons will continue the tradition.

Grandpa had of course witnessed death, whereas my granny just read about it by scouring the obituary columns in the *Derby Evening Telegraph* with unnerving enthusiasm.

"Good Lord!" she would exclaim, "Old Mr Leadbeters dead. You remember him don't you?"

"Not really" mumbled grandpa, who was not particularly interested.

"Yes you do" she insisted. "He married that woman from Cooper Street. You know the one with the withered arm. I don't know what she saw in him though. Everyone thought he was three sheets to the wind and I'd swear he only ever washed at Christmas and birthdays."

There would then be a silence as granny flapped the newspaper and chuntered to herself.

"Well I never! You remember Dougie Bailey don't you Len?" asked granny oblivious of grandpa trying to have forty winks.

"Who?" he muttered.

"Dougie Bailey. He had that little dog, you know, it only had three legs. You must remember him. He was married to, what's her name? She had that chip shop for a while near the park. Always had a runny nose and was forever sneezing over the battered cod."

"Can't say as I do" replied grandpa about to doze off.

"Well I remember him at Firs Estate School" announced granny. "He was a mucky little tyke, always putting his hand up your skirt and trying to kiss you. It was him that put that pet mouse down Doris Barlow's knickers. Screamed blue murder she did and then wouldn't let anyone near her to get it out. That was him alright. Dirty little devil."

Again all would go quiet for a while until granny spotted another person she knew and the silence would be shattered again as she shouted out the demise of yet another victim.

"I'll go to the foot of our stairs! I can't believe this Len."

"What now?" groaned grandpa having actually nodded off for a couple of minutes.

"It's Thelma Liveresage. She passed away last Friday. Who'd have thought it? I was only chatting to her last week outside the grocers. Mind you she didn't look quite herself. I said to her at the time I said you don't quite look yourself Thelma." Granny rattled on, "She was a lovely girl, always kept herself well. Had lovely hair, I say, she had lovely hair. Never knew why she didn't have that big mole taken off the side of her nose though. Lovely hair. You remember her husband Larry?"

"Larry who?" enquired grandpa, having now given up the idea of having a snooze.

"Larry Liverton you silly beggar. He used to do the Midnight Mail. I don't know how she put up with him smelling the way he did. Oooh, but she did have lovely hair."

I should explain here that the midnight mail was a euphemism for a particularly unpleasant job that was about as far removed from posting letters as you could get. It referred to the unfortunate souls that came during the hours of darkness to empty the contents of the outside lavatories. Most of my relatives lived among the many streets of 'jerry built' terraced houses which would have an access entry every so often to allow you to get along to the back of the houses and gardens. As the men carrying the buckets of sloppy excrement and attendant pong would be passing numerous back doors it was deemed too anti-social to be undertaken during the day, so it was carried out when everyone was presumably fast asleep in their beds. It must have been quite a hazardous job and spillage must have been a common occurrence on the lengthy trip back to the sewage lorry out in the street. My maternal granny's lavatory for example, was at the very bottom of her garden and the brick path to it, like many others was terribly uneven and it would be very easy to trip and find yourself in an unenviable and extremely whiffy position staggering about in the dead of night adorned with faecal offerings. It would need more than a bar of Lifebouy soap to shift that lot, and unlike the television advertisement no one would be coming up to you and whispering 'B O' in your ear. For the uninitiated 'B O' stood for body odour.

On the subject of my maternal granny, I tended not to visit her very often as I found her a little hard going and short on conversation, plus her house was rather dispiriting. The back room she lived in during the day sitting by a huge, polished cast-iron range always seemed to be gloomy and cheerless. The front room to the house was much sunnier and lighter but was never used and a three piece suite lay beneath dust sheets that I cannot ever remember being taken off. The door from this room led out onto the street and despite this entrance never being used my granny would still get down on her knees and religiously scrub and whiten the doorstep. This would have been a matter of pride in the old days and with granny I guess it was a case of tradition dying hard. There was not much else to be seen in the room except a couple of old vases on the mantelpiece and two large pictures hanging on the wall made to look like oil on canvas. They were displayed in ornate gold frames and depicted *Moses in the Bulrushes* and the *Entrance of the Queen of Sheba*. After granny died I took the Moses picture but never really knew what to do with it, so eventually it was consigned to the outhouse where it languished for a couple of years until its fate was finally sealed by my bicycle falling over and the handlebars making a sizeable hole in Moses's wicker basket. That was the end of the picture as indeed it would have been in reality for Moses who would have been lost for words (if he had not been too young to know any) at the site of my bicycle handlebars puncturing the side of his basket and would be wondering what the hell it was as he slowly sank and drowned. Had this been the case and he momentarily had a glimpse into the future then I reckon Moses would a have been a bit nettled knowing he would miss out on that amazing Red Sea trick he could have pulled off in later years. That last sentence needs a bit of thinking about as I am not quite sure how it would all have worked out. I guess that is just one of the many pitfalls in trying to re-write history.

By all accounts my maternal granny was born by Sadler Gate Bridge, was a well-dressed local beauty and married beneath her. Okay so my grandpa liked a beer or two most nights and was forever finding things that had fallen off the back of a lorry, or horse and cart, but it seems to me to be a tad harsh for a man whose entrepreneurial efforts were unappreciated. I only ever remember granny in a frilly mop cap (that's not to say she never wore any other clothes, you understand) and I cannot recall ever seeing her leave her house. Yet I know she did now and then wander down the road to the cemetery at the bottom of the street to keep the weeds down around her husband's grave. The thing is I have this image in my mind of granny in her mop cap like a Breugelian figure, bent over and slashing at the ground among the headstones with a Ghurka kukri which is precisely what she used. In the twilight it would have presented an alarming spectacle as though she was hacking and dismembering a body, thus giving rise to a possible newspaper headline reading, 'Mop Cap Murderer Strikes Again.' Her machete wielding antics were to keep the site clear for the day when she would be laid on top of her husband's coffin. Now, as it turned out after she had died and sometime during the period between her death and her funeral, someone was alerted to the fact that the original grave had not been dug deep enough and consequently granny's coffin was too high and would be sticking out above ground. This created quite a dilemma for either the coffin would have to be reduced in height, or granny would have to be flat-packed or put through a trouser press in order to fit. Fortunately, a brick-layer saved the day and added a row of bricks on the existing grave just in time for the funeral, otherwise we may all have been sitting around the graveside with some sandwiches, a flask of tea and having a bit of a sing-song waiting for the 'bricky' to add the extra layer before we could all go home.

Back on the home front my sister Sylvia's 'husband-to-be' Gerfried had quickly taken up residence in what had been my bedroom prior to me leaving home and almost before my mother had had time to change the sheets. Before I left home to get married sister Sylvia (sounds like a nun overseeing the 'fallen girls' in a Magdelana Sisters laundry) and I did not have a lot of contact as we were both working during the day and at weekends I would be out with my mates and she would be out with hers. More often than not, I would be climbing or caving in the Peak District and she would be bopping to a live band on a man-hunting night at the newly established Locarno in Babbington Lane. The bait apparently for man-hunting was stilettos, stockings, suspenders and an eye-watering pointy bra that actually threatened to take out an eye that may have got too close! According to my sister, lads at that time preferred the girls wearing stockings as they could get to grips with bare skin whenever they shoved a hand up the skirt (I say, that's a bit forward) of a prospective girlfriend. Presumably this either became a lingering erotic moment, or a sharp rejection followed by a smack across the face. My sister would stuff cotton wool into the pointed ends of her Triumph bra, so that after a passionate clinch (for clinch read grope) and snogging session the ends were not squashed flat giving her boobs the appearance of two partly deflated balloons. I suppose they named the bra Triumph because initially it looked like a maiming device and for any amorous lad to successfully get past and into it deserved a reward worthy of his triumphant victory. On reflection it was a pretty silly design as few, if any girls could have sported a natural pair of breasts that resembled two dunce's hats to fill the thing.

Preparation for the 'hunt' could start the day before with a hair washing session (I'm sorry I can't go out tonight, I'm washing my hair) followed by an invasion of rollers and metal clips stuck all over her head as she yielded to the rigours of a home 'perm' that had to stay in overnight and were in actual fact far too painful to sleep on. All this palaver resulted in my sister spending the night face down in bed inviting suffocation. But it only got worse as late Saturday afternoon approached there would be the energetic and torturous procedure of pushing bits of her body into a 'roll-on' corset and suspenders, bits that did not necessarily want to be pushed in and constrained for umpteen hours. I gather the 'roll-on' was a left-over from my mother's regime that had been instilled into my sister along the lines of, if she refused to wear the infernal device then after she had her first and any subsequent children her stomach would be down near her knees. This could be not only unsightly, but an irritant whenever she had occasion to wear wellingtons as her stomach might very well chafe on the top of her boots. Next came the full blouse, the stiff, tight-waisted petticoat looking like a multi-layered lampshade and perhaps a back-combed, bouffant, Bridgette Bardo, look-alike hairdo. The last of this exhausting ritual was the application of war paint, lipstick, blusher and mascara and I must not forget the liberal dustings of ubiquitous talcum powder somewhere along the line. Sister Sylvia was a slave to Max Factor. I seem to remember at that time we lads would laughingly chant the doggerel, *'Max Factor, knacker lacquer, adds lustre to your cluster.'* I am not entirely sure as to what it alluded to, but I thought I should mention it purely as an outstanding example of cultural social history, or is it just a silly smutty rhyme? When my mother was a young lady and applied rouge to her face before going out of an evening, her strict Victorian style father would consider it to be an unnecessary waste of time and referred to it in derogatory terms as 'monkey's arse dust' thus implying that at some time in his past he had actually been sufficiently close to observe a monkey's dusty rectum. Of course, nobody would have dared ask him. Shortly after tea my sister would leave to catch the bus into town and after we heard the front door slam, all that remained was a faintly visible toxic cloud of talcum powder and inflammable hairspray assaulting our nostrils and wafting through the rooms like mustard gas in a World War One trench. There was no mistaking Saturday nights in our house. As my sister often missed the last bus home because she was stuck to some lad's face or fighting off (or encouraging) a suspender 'twanger' it could be around midnight before the sound of the front door being slammed closed was heard again. This meant that often she did not surface much before the radio programme *Pick of the Pops* got underway on a Sunday afternoon and possibly looking the worse for wear.

Inevitably some of her victims actually made it to the front door of our house including a not very exciting chap who apart from being rather older than my sister was something of a culture vulture. Well, even I could see that was going nowhere, especially as she was playing fast and loose with the son of her boss at the same time. I mean to say, promiscuous or what? Then along came Rolf a young man from Switzerland who just happened to be an excellent rock climber. He came out a couple of times with me and showed me how not to fall off quite as often as we tackled an ascent of Ilam Rock in Dovedale. Now Rolf was what you might best describe as 'a bit of a lad' and appeared one night outside the house when everyone was in bed including my sister who refused to get up and see him. The conclusion to this scenario has always been mantled in mystery, but it is fairly safe to assume that he found his way to the back of the house and conveniently beneath my sister's bedroom window. It was now developing into a true Romeo and Juliet situation but without the serenading because my parents slept in the adjacent room and although they were used to the local moggies caterwauling and hedgehogs screaming mercilessly in the garden at night, I rather think that Rolf breaking into a full-blown session of Alpine yodelling might just have aroused their suspicions. In the absence of a balcony (what did you expect? This was a corporation house in Chaddesden not a wealthy pad in Verona!) Rolf climbed the drainpipe to gain access to my sister's boudoir where no doubt he did a bit more climbing, mainly into her bed and... well, you can guess the rest. I wonder if he was wearing lederhosen at the time, you know those fetching, skimpy leather shorts with braces and a silly pointy hat with a feather sticking out of it? Anyway, the thing is sister Sylvia has never admitted to the events that took place that night, but neither has she ever denied it! Ultimately, Rolf climbed out of the picture and my now, brother-in-law Gerfried's persistence paid off and he won her over with his bright red Triumph Roadster (this is not an innuendo) where she could be driven around playing the role of Faye Dunaway wearing a scarf, her hair blowing in the wind and looking all terribly 'Monte Carlo', until that is, disaster struck. Driving down Max Road one day some clown drove straight out of a side road and rammed into the Roadster. If ever there was a case for Specsavers then this was it, because you have to ask yourself, how on earth could you not see a bright red car with a quarter mile long bonnet (okay, so that's an exaggeration) coming down the road towards you? This beautiful machine met an inglorious end in a scrapyard and Gerfried, now a broken man would never view life in quite the same way ever again.

The time was at last drawing near to temporarily leave behind my family, my relatives, my childhood and my adolescence and move to the flat land of East Anglia. I had landed my first photographic post at a research station outside Huntingdon after being subjected to an interview by half a dozen boffins that knew next to nothing about photography. However, I thought they enjoyed my rather inappropriate example of my skills with a 10" x 8" transparency depicting an alluring, busty, leggy lass in a raunchy pose and suspected they only employed me in the hopes I might have some more to show them. Just how wrong could I be! It turned out most of them were so bound up with their research and their egos that had the girl in question suddenly leapt out of the transparency and erotically gyrated in front of them on the table, I doubt very much that it would have had any effect on them at all. I could feel already that this was not going to be a laugh a minute place to work, but the salary was worth having.

Lambretta Daze

The place where I now worked as a photographer was situated on the only area of elevated land for miles and gave a panoramic view of… well, not much at all really, except for a few church spires, some trees and fields stretching away to the edge of the world. The building had at some time in the past been quite a charming country residence with leaded windows and accessed from the road by a long tree-lined drive, while the south facing front had steps leading down to a sloping lawn and shrubberies. This is beginning to sound like some estate agents blurb; 'there are two bedrooms with power points and built-in wardrobes. The property also has a sizeable cellar and would suit the activities of a dominatrix'. The former description sounds idyllic until I mention the two double storey right angled wings which I would rate as nil on any architectural scale that had been attached to both sides of the original house at a much later date. A two-year-old child could have come up with something more acceptable, in fact I have seen better constructions in Lego! These were the main laboratories, but there were others scattered around the grounds containing all manner of scientific paraphernalia and serious looking men in white coats doing serious looking things. I consider it fortunate that I had my quarters in the old part of the house, my studio and office being stuffed into the attic rooms that also had access to the roof where I spent many a sunny lunchtime laid out on the tiles and out of sight from everyone. There was a smaller room behind a closed door from my studio which was rarely opened as wasps had taken up residence in there for much of the year and I for one was not about to go in and introduce myself. My darkroom was a small room in one of the awful laboratory wings and inconveniently down two sets of stairs including the grand flight into the reception hall. The window which would have overlooked the south facing garden had been blacked out, so with the light on or off I could have been in a room almost anywhere. This then, was my new empire and all I needed to do now was swot up on the techniques required for scientific photography, because my Diploma and training had been in creative photography and I really did not have a clue.

I quickly befriended a pipe-smoking lad from Yorkshire who worked in histology, had a creative mind and an uncontrollable mouth that was inclined to discharge a torrent of verbal sewage which rather made him unpopular among his fellow workers. In small doses he was good company and he often migrated from his laboratory to my office for a chat. He worked alongside a bearded, Scottish 'Rob Roy' lookalike and two girls, and when slicing specimens for microscopy got the better of him he would sneak off and amuse himself in the following manner. He would wait for one of the girls to go to the lavatory and then get into the maintenance passageway behind the loos. Once he had decided that the victim was well and truly settled on the seat and lost to the world in thought, he would push the ball-cock hard down in the cistern and give them a bit of a douche and also a surprise. It does beg the question, just what sort of mind lies behind that sort of amusement? Well, in this instance that sort of mind belonged to a man who was bald, wore thick lenses, had a maniacal grin and a pipe sticking straight out from the front of his face, and probably a man who had gone slightly demented through inhaling too much hot wax fumes from the specimen preparation vats. Of course he was far from alone in his idiosyncrasies (for idiosyncrasies read, weird, wacky, bizarre, cranky and oddball) for elsewhere shut away in their laboratories lurked other freaks who may very well have succumbed to the effects of their own experiments, or even been the end results of their own experiments.

Another person I got on well with was much older than me, a pathologist and the perfect absent-minded professor. His main field of work involved studying cancerous tumours and he was forever bringing gaping disembowelled carcasses to my studio for me to photograph the diseased organs. It does not take much of an imagination to guess how lovely they looked and smelt after an hour or so slowly cooking under a couple of hot spotlights. Nevertheless, he was a likeable fellow, forgetful and apparently permanently tired. A group of us would gather round his table at morning coffee break in the canteen simply for his entertainment value as one of his stranger facets was the eating of road-kills.

"What did you have for dinner last night Michael?" someone would ask.

"Err, what?" he would mumble, already starting to fall asleep.

"Dinner, what did you have for dinner?"

"Oh, right, yes dinner. Well I found this dead badger the other morning so I tried that. It was perfectly alright. I'd kept it in the fridge for a couple of days."

"Ughh, yeuk!" we would all respond in unison.

"It was fine, a bit strong tasting and a bit tough and stringy, but otherwise perfectly edible" he replied with a bemused smile as if unable to comprehend why we all thought eating a badger several days old was quite ghastly, and in fact eating anything that had been run over was quite ghastly. The thing is he ate all manner of corpses, crows, pheasants, blackbirds, foxes, in fact anything you care to mention seen dead on a roadside, Michael had probably eaten it.

"So what's next on your menu" someone would ask him.

"What!" a sleepy Michael would reply.

"What are you going to eat next?"

"Oh, next, well I found this… er…" and his eyelids would drop and Michael would fall fast asleep at the table. Perhaps five minutes later when we were all discussing another topic he would suddenly wake up and finish the sentence. "Er… dead hedgehog, looks alright to me. I'll try that tonight."

Obviously it paid to have an extremely important prior engagement should Michael ever ask you around for dinner, unless you are prepared for a possible dose of botulism and a week bent over double on the lavatory wishing you were dead. 'If only I'd known' would ring somewhat hollow on this occasion, because you had been warned.

Another of Michael's quirky obsessions, but less harmful to either himself or the rest of the human race concerned St Edmund, the one-time King of East Anglia who died in ad 869 so naturally they were not personally acquainted. Ed was captured during a battle in which his side lost and was tied to a tree and used for target practise by some not very nice chaps who stuck so many pointy sticks into Ed that he actually began to resemble Mr Hedgehog. When they got a bit bored of all this as well as getting annoyed at Ed's constant voicing of his beliefs, someone decided to shut him up for good by decapitating him and chucking his head into a nearby wood. Now if you think that had certainly done the trick, then you would be very wrong, because a little later along came some of Ed's aficionados shouting, 'Where are you friend?' to which the severed head from somewhere in a bramble patch replied 'Here, here!' Now you have to admit that is a pretty cool stunt. A talking head! Had he not been a man born before his time he could have easily got a starring role in *Pirates of the Carribean*. He certainly liked a bit of a jape did our Ed. It is quite unbelievable really, unless you have just rolled out of the pub smashed out of your head then you would believe anything. Anyway, Michael had hatched this plan to gather together St Edmunds relics which only amounted to a few odds and ends like a couple of bones, some teeth that had been knocking about in France and a pair of socks and have them ceremoniously floated up river to Cambridge on a kind of royal barge, or if funds were running a tad short, an inflatable air-bed would have to do instead. At this stage he had not yet worked out the logistics of getting St Edmund to Bury St Edmunds where he was to be interred, so it would have to be by taxi, or bus, or the relics put in a carrier bag and slung over the handlebars of a bicycle as Bury St Edmund is not too far away by bike. Somewhere down the line I got sucked into all this nonsense because Michael wanted photographs taken of images, sculptor and effigies of St Edmund that existed in various churches dotted about the Fens as evidence for his barmy scheme. Enter one duped photographer who really should have known better rising ridiculously early on a Saturday morning to spend a very long and very boring day photographing some very boring subjects, while Michael gabbled continuously about his master plan. As the day wore on I passed in and out of sleep occasionally tuning in to the ceaseless background drone of Michael's voice. They say every dark cloud has a silver lining and mine was that I had brought my own packed lunch and consequently I was not subjected to one of Michael's ring-ouzel sandwiches or whatever diabolical filling he was eating that day.

As an interesting and very apt footnote, St Edmund was the patron saint of pandemics. Now given Michael's penchant for eating manky roadside carcasses it would seem not too unreasonable to assume that he was more than capable of starting a future pandemic of cholera, smallpox, typhus, leprosy and should an outbreak of Bubonic Plague occur around the table at coffee time then we would all know exactly who had eaten flea-infested rat on a slice of toast for supper, and who to blame. You see, Michael and St Edmund had a lot in common and could have had a remarkable working relationship with Michael starting epidemics of pandemic proportions and St Edmund exercising his power as a patron showing sympathy to a populace covered in pustules and boils and dropping like flies. They could have been really good mates.

Perhaps one of the strangest inmates at the research station was a chap called Jeff who worked in a laboratory next to Michael, although quite what research Jeff was supposed to do I never discovered. Very little I suspect. His passion out of work was restoring vintage vehicles and he had a fair collection of old cars around his house including a Bull-nose Morris, a Riley and a Talbot with headlamps the size of dinner plates. One of Jeff's research projects was on a young woman who worked in another laboratory along the corridor who seemed hell bent on having an affair with someone and Jeff got the green light. One warm summer evening he found himself in a corn field with the woman in question lying on her back and thinking of England. Meanwhile, Jeff was getting over-excited in only his socks and managed an unsuccessful scrabble and fumble in the corn field, by which time the woman had either fallen asleep or was thinking not so much of England but actually of being somewhere else in England. Another time he came to work one bitter, cold frosty morning wrapped like a rolled up mattress and driving a three wheeled invalid carriage that he had recently purchased. Any sane person would have tried it out in warmer weather, but not Jeff, he had to try it now regardless of the arctic conditions. After the machine had spluttered to a halt in the car park, the blue-faced frozen bundle of coats and several pairs of trousers painfully made its way slowly and awkwardly down the driveway, clumping along as if someone had poured quick setting cement inside his clothes. His frozen face had failed to function several miles back down the road and did not even allow him to grimace. After disrobing in slow motion he spent the rest of the morning clamped to a radiator in an effort to thaw out. To my way of thinking, this venture of his bares the unmistakable hall mark of an unhinged mind and should you need further proof, read on. I had an occasion to live for a while in a flat belonging to Jeff, tagged on to the end of his house. It became part of life for me to observe Jeff on a summer evening, bound out of his house as though he had been in close contact with an electric cattle prod, rush into the garden and start piping away on a clarinet. Now this was no Benny Goodman, but he obviously fancied himself as a jazz player and was under the illusion that he had to play in the nip with only his shoes on. Yet again I proffer the theory that this is not normal behaviour and it was no Acker Bilk playing *Stranger on the Shore* but it was certainly strange Jeff playing in the nude and how much stranger can you get than that? Anyway, at least these whackos made life interesting in what was otherwise a staid, lack-lustre environment and if all else failed we could always ogle at the tall, perfectly formed figure of Wendy, a lab assistant who would walk down the driveway like a goddess, and who we all agreed was put together far better than any Airfix kit.

The type of work I was involved with was for the most part fairly uninteresting and trying. For example, to photograph a culture smudge or shadow in a petri dish full of Agar jelly (not to be recommended with ice cream) was akin to trying to get a picture of a smear on a pane of glass in full sunlight and far removed from being creative. The crackpots in white coats sometimes allowed themselves the occasional mild outburst of euphoria at the photographic results, but in the main they remained boringly 'egg-bound' in their ways and I considered much of it was a waste of both film and paper and I tried not to think too much about what ghastly and possibly deadly viruses they were polluting my studio with. One such researcher spent her time trying to perfect the ideal shape for a yolk when an egg is cracked open and I recall photographing dozens of eggs side on to aid her in her questionable efforts. With the best will in the world I have to pose the question, does anyone else really care what shape the yolk is once the egg is lying in a frying pan alongside two sizzling rashers of back bacon and a Derbyshire oat cake? Surely not, unless the yolk is square, or triangular, or shaped like a pyramid or a rhombohedral-decahedron (if such a thing exists) in which case you might just think twice about eating it for breakfast. Others studied the best way to house battery hens and keep them happy, healthy and egg productive. I could have provided the answer to that one by suggesting they leave the door open so the hens can get outside to scratch around freely in the open air, but nobody ever consulted me. I was just there to take photographs and prepare charts and graphs that showed the rise and fall of chicken droppings or some other equally mind-numbing criteria. You will have gathered by now that I was not overly enamoured of my duties, but as I said earlier on, it did put money in my pocket and this allowed me to up my transport status.

In my early days I would commute home to Derby on a Friday evening by train and return on a Sunday evening. Once winter had arrived the train journeys became tiresome and after hanging around for a connecting train to Huntingdon on the drab, dreary, dismal, draughty and dimly lit platform at Peterborough station on a Sunday night then the novelty, if there had ever been one quickly dissolved into the bleakness of the night. At Huntingdon I then had to wait for an unpredictable bus to take me to the village where I was boarding, finally collapsing on my bed in solitary confinement and trying to put out of my mind the Monday morning cycle uphill for another day in the scintillating (yawn) asylum with its head-cases and barmy experiments. The time had come for me to sell my trusty old steed and move onto something motorised to enable me to get to Derby and back more conveniently. Rick a young man housed on the nearby RAF camp answered my advertisement and we met for the transaction in the Three Horseshoes pub and downed a few beers before I handed over my Parkes cycle that had served me well. These expensive cycles are now considered to be vintage and consequently quite collectable, so I hope you are still looking after it Rick. We became good friends and I would spend time with him drinking at the RAF camp folk club which was held once a week where I would subject my ears to the sound of some lad twanging away on a guitar and moaning his way through a mournful and lamentable dirge about some fair maid who had *done me wrong* during a lover's tiff. This might be followed by someone else giving a rowdy and tuneless rendition of *American Pie* and everyone, it seems, wanted to be a Ralph McTell and 'take you by the hand and lead you through the streets of London' until it got to the stage where I was wishing that someone would take them by the scruff of the neck and lose them in some remote street of London. Still, the beer was cheap which made the whole experience marginally better than staying at home and watching television.

I now became the proud owner of a provisional driving license and I was all set to leap upon my maroon, metallic finish Lambretta 150 scooter and scoot off into the setting sun, except I had absolutely no idea how to drive the thing. Erring on caution I decided to have it delivered to my digs where there was a quiet country lane I could use to get to grips with the technique of operating the machine without the danger of killing anyone in the process. The man who delivered the scooter explained about starting it up, and then the brakes, clutch and changing gear then left me in a cloud of confusion to cope with the 'machine infernal'. I realised it was not going to be anything like my old bicycle and far more lethal. Somehow I had to get home to Derby that afternoon riding the thing as best I could. After stalling the engine umpteen times and wobbling all over the road narrowly missing wayside trees and telegraph poles I decided I was ready. I roared up the lane out of the village and up to the main road where I had to stop and of course stalled. This was going to be the familiar pattern that accompanied me most of the way home, brake, stall, into gear and stall, and so on, and so on, mile after mile after mile. In the failing light of a wintery afternoon I joined the very busy and suicidal Friday afternoon traffic on the A1 and headed north, stalling at every roundabout of which there seemed to be millions as I wobbled and wavered at a steady forty five miles an hour. Drivers could see my L plates and many beeped their horns and some shouted, but because of the roar of the traffic and me wearing a crash helmet I could not be sure what they were saying, but I think they were probably all very nice people just wanting to say 'Hello' to me. It took me awhile to find how to operate the lights which at least reduced the chances very slightly of me becoming a road traffic accident statistic too early on into my journey. I stopped and started and wobbled my way to the Stamford turn off, then stopped and started and wobbled my way through Oakham, Melton Mowbray (far too late to buy a pork pie and I was starving) and on to Nottingham. Somewhere down the Derby road I suddenly started to get everything synchronised and was able to stop and take off without the engine cutting out. By now my kick starter leg had become a gelatinous appendage that had fallen apart at the knee and thigh several hours ago and I was also feeling considerably drained with the effort and concentration of mainly trying to stay alive particularly on the A1 section of the journey. There had been too many times when I thought I was about to fall off fearing that no would spot me in the dark and I would become pancaked on the road with my face unattractively patterned by a variety of lorry tyre treads. At one point I had to stop for fuel which entailed putting two star petrol into my tank and then calculating from the side of a portable hand pump how much two-stroke oil to squirt into the petrol. It was all contributory to grinding me down so by the time I reached home a fortnight later, at least that was how long I felt I had been on the road, Carol had come to the conclusion that I had no idea where I was going and had probably crossed the Scottish border and was still going strong. I slept very well that night. The thing was that without any real warning I had entered the world of mechanical stratagems and the combustion engine and I were still complete strangers. Entering into the spirit of things I took the bit between my teeth and went out and bought an owners maintenance manual and a socket set costing me fourteen pounds and ten shillings. I still use it to this day. Nobody makes socket sets like that anymore.

Now that I had mobility I could wallow in the questionable delights of leaving Derby at six o'clock on a Monday morning in the snow and frost and ice to travel the two or hours it took me to arrive at my digs in time for breakfast. My landlady was very good to me in that respect and would never let me leave the house until I had waded through one of her mammoth breakfasts. Often I would arrive looking like Jeff had done on his invalid carriage, blue-faced, frozen to the bone and barely able to dismount from my scooter. I told myself this was much better than sitting for hours on a warm train with nothing to do except look out of the window and watch the countryside slip past. I am not really sure I convinced myself. After a couple of months of this we managed to sell the house in Derby and Carol moved down to a house I had bought in Godmanchester, got herself a job in a solicitors office in Huntingdon and early morning trips down the A1 became a thing of the past. That of course did not mean that danger did not lurk in the country roads of this quiet backwater and it was not long before I was initiated into my first attempt at flying. This was the result of going too fast around a corner whereupon the wobble set in and the Lambretta and I parted company. It headed sensibly onto the grass verge while I headed for the hard tarmac. This was to be a re-occurring pattern and I became convinced it had something to do with a safety device built into the scooter at the factory, because after a crash the scooter always ended up better off than I did. I think for my first attempt at flying I did quite well, whereas the landing was rubbish and I obviously needed to work on this aspect of a crash. Coming down to earth had been a painful experience and I noticed a gaping hole in the back of my trousers which allowed me to conveniently observe my bloodied hip covered in grit without the need to remove them and draw unnecessary attention to myself. Luckily it was a quiet Sunday afternoon and the only witness was a small boy who stood staring at me from the other side of the road. He finally asked, "Did you fall off mister?" I looked around to see if I could find something to hit him with, but fortunately for him there was nothing suitable. "Did you fall off mister?" he asked again. "Well what do you think?" I replied looking at him menacingly, after which he not only shut up, but also managed to achieve the impossible which was to appear even more gormless than ever. I picked up my recumbent scooter, started the engine and carried on my way back home. I quickly realised after my second crash which occurred on the A1 at night following a front wheel blow-out that it was impossible to stay on a scooter once the wobbles had set in and the only thing I could do was look forward to another few seconds of being airborne. After my first mishap my doctor took one look at my bleeding hip and simply suggested I pick the bits of road out and slap on a burn dressing and all would be well. However, the most horrendous incident that still makes my toes curl whenever I think of it happened not long after I had passed my scooter driving test.

I took the test, such as it was, one morning in Peterborough and after a few questions on the Highway Code, most of which I managed to give a different answer to the one the examiner was expecting, he sent me off on my scooter saying he would jump out at some point during the circuit to test my reactions for an emergency stop. True to his word he appeared as if from nowhere and leapt out from a line of parked cars, whereupon I braked hard and much to my surprise neither of us died. The whole thing seemed a pretty daft idea to me and I would not mind betting he was a familiar face at the local A & E department. I remember a girl at work telling me that when she took her moped test the week before me she was also subjected to the same scenario, except the examiner never leapt out from anywhere and she failed to find the test centre again, so she just went home. My memorable disaster took place on a Monday morning during the rush hour traffic on the hectic Cambridge road. Strapped onto my pillion was a black case containing the works expensive Nikon camera and lenses that I had borrowed (without permission) for the weekend. I set off at speed because I was running late and soon found myself among very heavy traffic. I decided to overtake a long lorry and moved alongside. Unfortunately he seemed to be going faster than I had anticipated and when I was about three quarters of the way along its length trying to race it on full throttle which would have been around seventy miles an hour, another lorry came from nowhere bearing down on me on the other side of the road. He got horribly close, horribly quickly and I remember thinking to myself that this was not looking too good and I did not have the power to successfully overtake. The oncoming lorry was flashing his lights and hitting the horn and I am sure I could make out the squashed flies on his radiator grill, and as the words 'lorry sandwich' flashed through my mind I knew that in seconds I would be joining them as a rather messy radiator mascot. Braking sharply at this speed would either send me wobbling into the oncoming lorry, or wobbling beneath the rear wheels of the lorry alongside me. When you assess the situation in the cold light of day then the two wobbling options were pretty grim and either would result in death. The gap between the two lorries decreased at a pant-wetting rate and I knew I was going to die. I glanced quickly over my shoulder and fancy

I saw a macabre figure riding pillion wearing black flowing robes, a black hood and grinning horribly. He was not a good looker and neither was he a natty dresser, and why was he carrying a scythe over one shoulder, and where had he come from and perhaps even more pertinent where were we going together? Instinctively I braked and predictably the stroppy scooter went in to the all too familiar 'Lambretta Wobble Waltz' and somewhere in the midst of the ensuing cacophony of roaring engines, flashing lights and squealing brakes I died. So, I hear you ask the question, who is writing this book? Well, the thing is at the precise moment when I gritted my teeth wondering whether to wet myself or not, everything went black. There was not even time for my life to flash before me, which was a bit of a shame as there would have been quite a few bits I would not have minded seeing again. Anyway, the next thing I was aware of in my dazed state was a voice asking me if I was okay and what an idiot I was. As I vaguely focussed on the world I could see my scooter in its usual position, lying on its side on the verge with the engine chuntering away to itself. I assumed the man who had spoken to me had presumed I was not dead and got into his car and drove off leaving me wondering why I was not dead. Unless of course, and this is a tad presumptuous of me that somewhere in heaven (I should be so lucky) there was an identical section of road carrying rush hour traffic to, well heaven knows where! I picked myself up and a severe pain shot down my leg and I saw that the same old scooter wound on my hip had been torn open yet again and was full of grit with blood trickling down into my socks. I could not help but notice that my backside was also on show as most of my trouser seat had been ripped off. Of course having pieces of your anatomy on show through ripped clothes was to become the fashion in later years, but for the moment I was ahead of my time. I limped to where the scooter lay and suddenly remembered the camera case. Luckily apart from a bashed in corner it was intact and still attached to the pillion, so I guess that guy in black must have sat on it and maybe squashed the corner. 'Oh! Praise be to the inventor of stretchy, elasticated luggage straps. You saved me from immediate unemployment.' I picked up the scooter and the engine cut out and simply refused to start. I had neither the will or the energy to try and kick-start it more than half a dozen times as my body ached all over and the pain of my leg throbbed in my head like a faulty out-board motor. There was no alternative but to push the thing the one and a half miles back home with a cooling breeze whistling around my nether regions. On reaching the house I shoved it into the garage (the scooter that is, not my nether regions) washed the grit out of the wound, slapped on two burn dressings and went to bed. Many times over the decades have I pondered over that day and cannot for the life of me figure out just how I survived that lorry sandwich and not end up spread-eagled on the radiator grill of the oncoming lorry, or for that matter, not finish up flap-flapping around the rear wheels of the lorry I was alongside. I can only think that my mind instantly shut down as it did not want to witness, or even be around when the inevitable seemed upon me. It has to go down as one of life's conundrums, but I have to say that I am very pleased about the remarkable outcome.

Shortly after this a German friend from work called Brigetta insisted in a demanding Teutonic manner that she should have a go on my scooter because it really could not be that difficult to drive. I told her how to operate the brakes and clutch and stood back. She put it into first gear, roared across the road at a disconcerting speed, mounted the pavement and hit a low brick wall full on. This catapulted her impressively over a high garden hedge and a dull thud followed by a gasping wheeze bore testament to the fact that 'the eagle had landed', or in this case that Brigetta had landed in somebody's flower bed. Clearly she had never been trained by the Luftwaffe. She was not best pleased about this turn of events and stormed out of the garden with an 'angry camp commandant' look about her and immediately set about blaming me for what had happened. She could be very short tempered. Her first day at the research station, for example, had almost tested it to the limit. She was put to work in the library department and her fellow worker was a French woman. Brigetta had a rather frosty reception because the French woman immediately launched into the story of how during the war she had worked for the Resistance and had been captured then interrogated by the Gestapo who had caused her excruciating agonies and left her with nothing to chew in the way of nails on her finger ends. Naturally, this put poor Brigetta in a bit of a spot because although she was undeniably German, it did not necessarily mean she had worked for the Gestapo and was going to carry on where they had left off by removing the French woman's toe-nails. They did become good friends after the 'don't mention the war' barrier had gone up and worked alongside each other quite happily. After the 'human rocket woman' episode which had not done the front of my scooter any favours I was beginning to think that the Lambretta's days were numbered and quite possibly mine along with it, so I sought the safety of four wheels and bought an old 1952 Series 1, Land Rover. I finally became the holder of a full driving license. However, it seems that the Lambretta will never entirely be forgotten as the taught skin over the scar still itches like crazy now and then and this is over forty years on.

The problem with this area of England is not only is it boringly flat, but most of the population, especially the young were at a loss as to how to spend their leisure time and it was generally accepted that there were only three choices, which was watch television, get drunk, or have sex in whichever order you preferred or was available to you. Many girls for example on a Saturday night would hang around the main entrance of the American air base just up the road in the hope of being picked up and taken inside to where there was a cinema, clubs and dancing, all social activities that did not exist elsewhere in the area. Naturally there was a price to pay for this, but most girls were quite happy to make themselves available for extra social activities if the situation required it, and it usually did. In contrast the RAF camp also nearby had virtually nothing to offer in the way of entertainment, so with many husbands being away a lot of the time restless, frustrated wives tended to go out and play with whoever was around to play with. About this time and getting tired of so called scientific photography I decided to address the situation by turning my garage into a photographic room and first up to model in my home-made studio was a young girl I called Mistress Higgins who had been sent round by her mother in an effort to curb her daughter's boredom. She was a petite, busty lass who wanted to pose in skimpy outfits and was happy to do so for a packet of twenty cigarettes and a few prints of herself. All went well for a couple of weeks or so until one night I drove her back to her house and she asked me in for a coffee. Because I knew her parents vaguely I thought it would be a sociable thing to do. As it turned out her parents were tucked up in bed and fast asleep. Suddenly and without any warning Mistress Higgins shoved me onto a sofa in the sitting room, placed a chair against the door, leapt on me and proceeded to snog me stupid before pushing a breast into my face. Well, I must say, it was an unexpected turn of events finding myself pinned down between her sturdy young thighs with a firm ample breast pressed into my face, which in itself was pleasant enough apart from the fact that she was wearing a black woolly sweater which was filling my nostrils with fluff. Helpless as I was (well, you would be wouldn't you?) when I was allowed to come up for air I became gripped by an outburst of sneezing which rather took the edge of things as well as spraying the front of her jumper with bits of mucous and damp fluff. My close encounter with her beating bosom quickly came to an end as she wiped herself down and I was forced to make rogue elephant impersonations blowing my nose into my handkerchief. Just as I was thinking that her next move might be to present me with a de-fluffed version (which I promised myself not to sneeze over) I realised that the moment was lost and I was shown the door, and in a mildly confused state drove home. Oddly enough I never saw much of her after that fleeting moment of lust and she never posed for me again.

I never did figure it out and shortly afterwards another situation arose concerning a married woman off the RAF camp who worked at the research station. We were quite good friends and she often came to my office or studio at lunchtimes for a chat although the conversations always seemed to be heavily laced with innuendos of a suggestive nature. This particular lunchtime she appeared to be pretty much her normal self, hanging around my studio being perhaps more sexual in her mannerisms than usual. I did not take too much notice as I was rather busy and announced that I had to get some films processed in a hurry at which point she disappeared. A few minutes later I went downstairs to my darkroom, closed the outer door, opened the inner door and switched the light on. Imagine my astonishment to see her there sitting on a worktop with a smile on her face and completely naked. It was blindingly obvious by the expression on her face that she was thinking to hell with processing your film I want you to process me. Once again I was caught off guard because it was lunchtime and I had not even got around to eating my sandwiches, yet here was this woman without a stitch on offering me her attributes as the lunchtime menu and clearly 'rutting like a stoat' to use a country saying. By now I was of the opinion that someone must be putting something in the canteen tea as seemingly innocent looking young girls as well as married women were metamorphosing into nymphomaniacs which was becoming highly, and not altogether unpleasantly, distracting! Life in general was becoming iniquitous and I needed to escape back to Derbyshire at least for the weekend in the interests of my own salvation. If only I'd known I was backing a loser and would be sought out like a rabbit down a hole being harassed by a ferret.

My wife and I were slowly drifting apart as she was mixing socially with many of her clients having soirees and sophisticated meat-loaf dinner parties while I diligently pursued my outdoor activities. I had spent several weekends in the Mendip caves after crossing England on my Lambretta on a Friday night from work and arriving some six hours later in Priddy just before closing time, and here I had met a group of cavers from Liverpool who all possessed that legendary whacky Liverpudlian brand of humour. They were great fun to be with and soon I was heading north on a Friday night to Derbyshire as this was a lot nearer for both of us and I had the ideal place to stay.

It was a small cottage situated on a very high exposed point overlooking Miller's Dale with amazing panoramas in all directions. It had once been a farmhouse and had a hay barn attached which was still in use. Whenever I opened the door to let myself in I was always greeted by the same smell of damp mustiness and leaking Calor gas. Inside was a black cast iron range and oven, a single gas lamp and in the kitchen a two ring gas cooker. The remainder of the place was lit with oil lamps or candles provided I could find anything dry enough to strike a match on once the matchbox itself had succumbed to the constant damp air. The water supply came directly from an open butt outside that collected rainwater off the stone slab roof, while across the yard a stone building housed the 'thunder box' reeking of a heady mixture of Elsan toilet chemical and ancient faeces that were long overdue for a hillside burial. I had spent many weekends here (in the cottage that is, not the reeking loo) in the past with mates, climbing, caving, drinking and sitting around the fireside swopping tales. During the era of the Liverpool cavers, work duties meant we were not able to get to Derbyshire until about lunchtime Saturday where we would all meet in The Waterloo for a few pints. I recall one winter we had met up and trudged through the snow to the cottage where we lit the fire and gathered around getting pleasantly barbequed at the front and unpleasantly chilled at the back. At around seven o'clock after it had been dark for about three hours we decided to go caving and ventured outside into the cold night and drove over to a hole named P8, a wet, sporty little cave not far from the head of Winnat's Pass. With water streaming into the short drop of an entrance you tend to get quite wet from the start and likewise on the way out, although by that time you are soaked to the skin anyway so it has little effect. However, in the black of night with a freezing wind cutting across the hillside we found that trudging back in the snow over the fields was a cooling experience to say the least. Before I had gone very far my wet hair had frozen to the collar of my wetsuit and to the back of my helmet as I plodded alongside my mates re-considering whether at that particular moment in my life collecting beer mats seemed a more preferable pastime. On the other hand we were, to resort to modern parlance, well hard! The most important thing was that we were all back at The Waterloo before closing time for another couple of pints before heading back to the cottage and a damp bed.

The link between the cottage and life in East Anglia came from an unexpected quarter after a teacher who had been a client of my wife (at her office in case you were thinking she was on the game) asked if I could show some slides of my past caving experiences to a group of students to see whether any of them might be interested in a weekend beneath Derbyshire. The response was overwhelming (that's how desperate they were to escape the flatlands for a time) and for some of them it would be a real treat because they had never seen a proper hill or a gorge before, never mind being under one. A weekend was decided on and about a dozen or so students signed up to put their lives in the hands of myself and my two best caving mates from Liverpool. We were after all, merely three experienced cavers with no knowledge whatsoever of taking school parties on an activity weekend, so all the parents were required to sign a waiver that exempted us from any blame should somebody not come back, except for one parent who was prepared to give us a back-hander if we could lose his son somewhere down a hole. Among the party were three teachers. One a quirky French lecturer who bought his jolly wife along, another a super fit PE instructor who was not too keen on confined spaces, and the third an unpredictable music teacher who came along for the walk. On the appointed day, this disparate bunch of lads, girls and teachers drove up the A1 in the grammar school mini-bus with the misguided blessings of the headmaster. How we all fitted into that tiny Tardis of a cottage is as mysterious as why does buttered toast always land butter side down, or why is it not possible to tickle your own feet, lick your own elbow, and why is there only ever one sock from a pair that comes out of the washing machine? Everyone was allotted tasks and shortly an edible but totally unidentifiable giant saucepan of splodge was bubbling and steaming on the gas rings, producing even more condensation on the walls and giving off an aroma not dissimilar to burnt milk and old pants. By now we were all starving hungry and I guess a hearty bowl of burnt milk and old pants would set us up a treat, and hopefully not be followed by an uncontrollable rush to the little building outside in the yard! The three of us bagged the only bedroom with three beds and the rest of the rooms where filled with bodies lying everywhere in sleeping bags so that it resembled a temporary disaster centre and nobody was interested in sleeping. A couple of hours later and with no sign of the talking, laughing and giggling abating the unexpected happened. The normally quiet and self-controlled music teacher decided he could stand the noise no longer and in a very loud voice that in the dead of night may very well have echoed over the dales and been picked up in Buxton by any amateur radio ham, yelled out "Will you all f.....g shut up and for f...s sake go to sleep". Well, you could have heard a pin drop as his unprecedented outpouring of expletives shocked the noisy students into immediate silence. They would never again see their music teacher in quite the same light.

Cometh the morning, cometh the tea, and in our case we three agreed we would not get out of bed unless we were served tea by a gorgeous, athletic, and highly intelligent blonde-haired girl who just happened to be the sixth form pin-up over which all the boys drooled at the very sight of her. And what a fine figure she cut later that same day in a black, skin-tight wetsuit. As an outstanding example of truth being stranger than fiction, some years later that young voluptuous girl who was called Annie who had brought me tea in bed that morning ended up being my second wife. Now you did not expect that did you? I was rather surprised myself! The weekend got underway with half of the group walking, while the other half were subjected to the dubious delights of a muddy Carlswark Cavern with its half sump. Then the next day the groups would change places. That Saturday night in The Waterloo after the first trip underground, the bar was filled with a gaggle of underage drinkers telling more exaggerated tales than you would hear at an anglers fishing convention in an attempt to scare the pants of the group who had yet to sample a day underground. The tales of subterranean bravado became quite excruciating so the teachers concluded that the best course of action to take was to secretly judge who had been the worst offender and reward them with the unenviable task of digging a large pit and emptying the contents of the lavatory into it. With so many people at the cottage the primitive loo, normally given a wide berth if possible had never been so popular, or so full, or so stinky and consequently it had developed a sort of 'prima donna' status for it demanded almost constant attention having only a small bucket and neglect would have created a fairly unapproachable overspill. Overall, the weekend had been a success and others followed, but as we three gathered in the pub for a farewell drink after everyone else had departed for home our conversation predictably turned to the memorable attractions and merits of Annie, the young blonde tea girl.

'Entente Cordiale,' Yeah right!

After three years in East Anglia, Carol and I separated and filed for a divorce. She stayed with her job, with the house, her cat and her penchant for eating tomatoes (don't ask) and latched on to a male client from work and entered a new chapter of her life. I left work at the research station (Hurrah!) and with a few possessions stacked in the back of a new Land Rover I had bought, I headed back to Derby with a young but legal Annie in the passenger seat, for we were also embarking upon another chapter in life. For some time now we had been planning a lengthy overland trip to Australia and we arrived at my parent's house in Chaddesden with our heads spinning with ideas and two bulging folders stuffed with information on countries from Africa, to Burma, to Singapore and beyond. We already had some visas along with some invites from a number of embassies and road construction companies offering us Land Rover spares should we need any. The first snag we hit was a refusal from the Burmese government to allow us to cross their border, their excuse being that crossings were in remote places, un-manned and the old World War Two military roads, which were the only way in were impassable. What they were really saying was they did not care too much for the English or anyone else much and would we keep out. I take the point about the tracks being bad news as I think the last people who had passed that way had been a group of student chaps from Oxford and Cambridge who took two Land Rovers through in the fifties on a massive 32,000 mile round trip to Singapore and back. This happened only twelve years after the war and it was hard going then with numerous bridges down and invasive jungle growth. The Burmese highways department if they had such a thing had been inexcusably neglectful! Next a famine started up in Mali and surrounding countries and we were advised to keep well away for fear of being attacked and our supplies stolen along with the possibility of finding ourselves on the menu as well. We had hoped to cross from the African continent to Aden but again we were warned off as the Yemen was unstable and Oman had hordes of bandit tribesmen that could ambush us and permanently inter us in a shallow sandy grave which would be most inconsiderate as we had a dinner date at the embassy in Kuwait which we would have to forgo. The thing is we were constantly being beset by obstacles and it made us start to think that perhaps a day at Skegness might be a lot less trouble and we could pretend we were crossing the Sahara by driving about on the beach. As this is my third reference to 'Skeggy' I think I should redeem myself by saying that I have not got it in for the place as it is a world famous seaside resort and in many ways epitomises what the British seaside is all about. It really took off after the brilliant piece of promotion in 1908 of a railway poster displaying a fat, jolly fisherman prancing around flapping his arms in a somewhat camp manner extolling the virtue that 'Skegness is SO bracing' as indeed it can be with a chill wind screaming in off the North Sea as you bravely venture onto the sand in your knitted swim-suit.

Undaunted, we continued to prepare the Land Rover in the street outside my parent's house. I made a collapsible bed for the back, installed a cooker, built two lockers for food and clothes, while my mother pitched in making mattress covers and some nice black curtains which gave a funereal look to the vehicle. One particular afternoon I was fitting a heavy steel support across the inside roof of the cab to aid supporting the six jerry cans sitting above it. I was drilling a hole with a half-inch bit when it suddenly slipped off. I had been pressing down on it very hard and as I lurched forward I smacked my face on the doorframe and dropped the drill onto my lap. Regrettably, the drill switch was on lock so it just kept on drilling firstly through my corduroy trousers and then into my leg. Luckily the ripped trouser leg got wound around the bit and stopped it drilling any further into my leg, but not enough to slow the drill which quite quickly began to tear my trouser leg further and work its way up to an area that did not want to be caught up in a drill. This, you understand, was an area that was far from redundant and its painful loss could not be compensated for by a career change as a castrato in a choir somewhere. I decided it was time to panic. "ANNIE!! Pull the b....y plug out, quick!!" Although totally unaware of my dilemma she reacted without hesitation and saved the day as the drill bit had just begun to chew the edge of my underpants. Another few seconds and I would have been spending the rest of my life with a squeaky, high-pitched voice and pandering heavily towards my new found feminine side, and what would be the chances of the local job centre finding me a position as a eunuch? Despite this near mishap and our arms throbbing with inoculations we were ready to go and seek some adventure abroad.

This was to be only my second time abroad as I had been to France the year before on a thwarted caving trip with the Liverpool lads which came to a grinding halt in a campsite at Payrac when the rear spring of our van snapped in two. My memorable contribution was to collapse by a roadside one afternoon in stomach griping agony followed by a visit to 'le docteur.' Now this is where I began to regret not paying sufficient attention during all those French lessons I had had at school, for despite the best part of four years studying I could barely string a couple of words together. When I was aged nine I recall learning my first foreign word by realising that the word 'Wassertank' written on the box containing a new tin water tower for my Hornby clockwork train set must mean water tank. Sadly, my grasp of languages hardly got beyond this point. Of course nowadays almost anything you purchase is accompanied with an 'Important Read this First' leaflet that will contain instructions on how to operate say, your newly purchased steam iron. This leaflet using half a tree in paper comes in practically every language under the sun apart from Ancient Egyptian hieroglyphics and possibly Aztec Nahual, the latter as we all know being a 'complex morphology characterised by polysynthesis and agglutination.' Actually, I have not the faintest idea what that means either! Anyway, my friend Terry accompanied me to the surgery for everyone was under the impression that he could speak a little French, whereas in actual fact he just happened to be the only one with a French language phrase book which would probably seal my fate. This is because experience of such books later on in life has taught me that they are full of mind-boggling interpretations which for the most part require you to be in the most unlikely circumstances for them to be of much use. Would you, for example ever need to utter 'J'ai perdu ma chaussette a la gare.' 'I lost my sock at the station' or perhaps when ordering food, 'Vous servez la chat curry?' 'Do you serve curried cat?' And let us not forget 'Mon parapluie a ete frappe par une mouette!' which would be invaluable if indeed your 'umbrella had been hit by a seagull.' 'Je veux un gynocologist' I really don't think so!

We sought out a doctor in a nearby town and I waited my turn. Shortly a door opened and a thin man wearing a thin moustache and large spectacles motioned us to enter his inner sanctum.

"Votre Monsieur de problem?" he enquired in a particularly disinterested manner.

"Stomach pain" I answered picking up on the word problem.

"Douleur abdominale?" he questioned looking out of the window at something outside in the street.

"What did he say?" I asked Terry who was thumbing through the medical section of his phrase book.

"Pardon, Monsieur" I replied.

"Abdominale! Abdominale!" he reiterated somewhat impatiently, jabbing a finger into his own stomach.

"Qui, qui, vomiting" I answered, mimicking a mock retch as the penny dropped. So far so good I was thinking until the doctor turned on me and said in a somewhat curt and almost threatening way.

"Veuillez enliver vos pantolons"

"What's he saying now?" I asked Terry who was turning the pages of his book like a man possessed.

"Ah!" Terry suddenly exclaimed, "Trousers."

"What about trousers."

"I think he wants you to drop your trousers" replied Terry with a grin.

The doctor was tugging at my trouser leg in an obvious effort to speed things up a bit. I did as requested but the doctor continued by tugging at my underpants.

"I think he wants you to drop your kecks as well." Terry chuckled enjoying every minute of my predicament.

"What for?" I answered somewhat concerned.

"Votre posterieur, plait" chipped in the doctor. "Votre derriere" he snapped.

"I think he wants to see your arse" replied Terry trying to control his sniggering.

"But I don't want to show him my arse. The pain is in my stomach not my arse" I protested.

"Sur le divan" ordered the doctor slapping a hand down hard on a couch.

With my trousers around my ankles and my pants around my knees I reluctantly climbed onto the couch. I feared for my 'derriere' as it was very apparent that 'le docteur' was not greatly enamoured of the English and I was in a highly vulnerable position; a position I may add that the doctor took full advantage of by unceremoniously ramming a large and cold thermometer up my rectum. Terry was having great trouble in controlling his laughter and the doctor was plainly becoming exasperated by the pair of us. After I had lain for a couple of minutes like an uncooked kebab with the thermometer sticking out of my backside the doctor without any warning yanked it out as if he was pulling a trapped toe out of a bath tap.

"Vous avez l'intoxication alimantaire. Tres mal" uttered the doctor.

"Is he saying I've been poisoned?" I asked Terry. But before he could answer the withdrawing of the thermometer had caused my intestines full of gas to release a long lingering hissing sound, pitched somewhere around middle 'C' I would say at a guess, which took us all by surprise. My immediate thought was that I had been punctured. I was highly embarrassed as we all dealt in our own way with the reeking stench that consumed all of us in the doctor's surgery. I really did have a 'tres mal' and gaseous stomach. I pulled my trousers back up and the doctor handed me some white powder (after the ordeal I had just put him through it was probably arsenic) and gesticulated that I should mix it with water, drink the concoction and then sleep which he motioned by putting his head on his hands. I assume that is what he meant, or maybe he was despairing at the linguistic inabilities of the two English idiots that had ruined his afternoon and fouled his surgery.

That night back at the camp another embarrassing situation occured, although I have never let on until now! All of the lads, bar one went on a clandestine night trip with a local caver who said the landowner did not allow cavers into this particular hole, so the only way it could be explored was when he was in his bed. Seems reasonable to me. Jim was the one who stayed behind because it appears that Maria his on, off, on, off, girlfriend was also staying despite them not having spoken much to each other since leaving Liverpool. I had been put to bed to sleep off my ailment when the pair of them came into the tent clearly fired up and determined to break the stony silence that had existed between them. I of course was supposed to be asleep and they, of course thought I was asleep. After some pretty corny chit-chat the breathing became heavy followed closely by some frantic clothes rustling.

"We can't do it here" announced Maria, "What if he wakes up?"

"He won't wake up, he's ill" replied Jim not wishing to miss the moment. More shuffling, grunting and sighing followed until everything suddenly stopped.

"Oh God!" exclaimed Maria, "You've broken my zip you clumsy sod."

"I didn't do it on purpose" protested Jim

"Well don't be so rough. I'll take my bra off myself or you'll bust that as well."

There followed more rustling of clothes and the sound of another zip being undone and more heavy panting, gasping and flesh slapping as they both neared boiling point. Having listened to all this going on I decided that now was the time to play my hand. As all the expletives gushed forth in a crescendo of "Oh s...!, Ooogh f...!, oh God!" I coughed a couple of times, mumbled something incoherently, turned over in my sleeping bag and pretended to go back to sleep. That was more than enough to stop the pair of them dead in their tracks with the effectiveness of throwing a bucket of cold water over a pair of copulating dogs in a street. Okay, so it was mean of me, but I felt I had suffered an indignity at the hands of the doctor which I needed to avenge, and anyway it had not been much of a fun day until now. All ended well for Jim and Maria as they were friends with each other once more, at least for the remainder of the trip.

Annie and I left Derby very early one morning to catch the ferry to France. We drove south for several days enjoying the freedom, the sunshine and fresh croissants. One morning with a bag full of hot croissants we pulled off the road to enjoy them with some butter and jam when an old French granny dressed completely in black and resembling a rather large crow came wandering along the road. She paused in front of us, gave us a toothless grin, said something unintelligible and continued on her way. She had only gone about ten yards when without warning she hitched up her skirts, squatted down and defecated oblivious to either us or the passing traffic. She calmly arose, adjusted her clothes and wandered off as the flies moved in. It was a breakfast treat we could have done without. We explored gorges, valleys, Roman ruins and slept in the Land Rover wherever we could park for a night, which as it sometimes turned out was not always the wisest of choices. Early one evening I drove into Avignon to see the famous bridge of the equally famous song *Sur le pont, d'Avignon* covered in lights which made it look quite pretty as they reflected in the river. Unfortunately we never actually got onto the 'pont' as intended due to me taking a wrong turn in the dark and into a narrow side street strung with low balconies and even lower washing lines. The street suddenly became alive with lots of people shouting things like 'L'Anglais stupide' and 'Batards Anglais', which even I could tell were not friendly greetings inviting us to come inside their homes and share a glass of wine. I think they got a tad overwrought by the balcony I chipped with the roof-rack, the potted plant I knocked over on the pavement and the full line of washing I ran into that snapped and fluttered to the ground except for a blouse that had snagged on a jerry can and was not discovered by us until the following morning. Still, it could have been a lot worse had the owner still been wearing it at the time!

We cut along the Mediterranean coast to the south, along the flashy promenade at Cannes and past beaches displaying acres of sun-bronzed flesh lying about like scores of Arbroath 'smokies'. Some even had two poached eggs on top. From here we headed north into the foothills of the

Alps and were almost overturned by a very gusty Mistral wind as we drove along a rather exposed mountain ridge. We went for the Italian border crossing at a remote place called Isola 2000 which was to be a ski resort but still in the early stages of construction. In future years it would be frequented by the good, the bad and the posers who would flock here to show off their gaudy coloured outfits, trendy cutting edge shades and clump around in the equivalent of over-sized deep sea diver's boots. And then there would be the phonies who spend hours loafing about at a table on the open veranda downing Pimms No1 like there was no tomorrow, wearing woolly bobble hats and sweaters far worse than anything you might have been given at Christmas, hand knitted by a doting aunt. It is here on the veranda that the skiing version of the angler's tale takes place. One such person, for example, would be Mr Boring sat at a table with a leg in plaster attracting (for attracting read, snaring innocent victims who afterwards might find themselves feeling suicidal) the attention of any unwary prey. He would tell you that he had been skiing 'off piste' despite being warned of the danger of avalanches. Of course Mr Boring's philosophy was if you are not living on the edge then you are taking up too much space, (groan). Anyway, there he was roaring downhill at well over seventy miles an hour when he unexpectedly lost a ski on an extremely difficult turn. Unfazed and being an expert snowboarder which goes without saying, but Mr Boring is going to tell you anyway, he continued at high speed on one ski skilfully negotiating his way through a dense pine forest and past some jagged rocks before finding himself above an awesome drop over which he launched himself. Mr Boring clearly had nerves of steel, which again goes without saying, but he will tell you that as well. He was found shortly after by a slobbering St Bernard dog owned by two men in the ubiquitous pointy hats and lederhosen who just happened to be nearby getting in some practice on their alpine horns. They became so excited by their rescue that they went into raptures of yodelling and danced about slapping each other's thighs. In truth the credit should have gone to the sniffing power of the St Bernard, but no one seemed inclined to slap the dog's thighs. At this point the unfortunate listener will either be speechless with awe and admiration, or as is more likely to be the case, will have gone to sleep and fallen off their chair. The real story is that Mr Boring had never actually got any further than the nursery slopes in the morning after which he spent the entire afternoon getting thoroughly plastered at the hotel bar. Eventually, and somewhat the worse for wear, Mr Boring had staggered upstairs to his room with an incredibly overfull bladder, let himself into his room but in his rush to reach the bathroom had tripped over the edge of a rug and knocked himself out on the doorframe. When he finally came around he discovered he had a broken ankle and some very wet trousers. The thing is that far-fetched though this tale may seem, you can bet that at another table not too far away an even more fanciful and unbelievable story is unfolding that again will leave some hapless soul questioning the purpose of their life and wondering how long it would take to stab themselves to death with their own ski pole. Isola 2000 had all this waiting for it in the near future, but for the moment it was simply a few scattered huts, concrete foundations and piles of bulldozed earth.

We crossed the area of no man's land between the two borders and arrived at the Italian side early evening. This mountainous outpost consisted of a man and a hut, or to be more correct, a man closing a hut as his day had finished and he was about to disappear down the steep valley road and home, and in all probability to a steaming plate of spaghetti and a bottle of vino Rosso. Not surprisingly he was somewhat miffed to see an overladen Land Rover lumbering towards him. He stepped out and stopped us and we both got out.

"Buona sera" we said with a smile. We had been practising that greeting from our phrase book so we could feel like real Italians.

"Buona sera" he replied rather sternly. "Passaporto per favour" he demanded holding out his hand. He flicked through the pages, gave us both a cursory glance and handed them back. Fingering the flap on his gun holster (was he contemplating shooting us for having turned up so late?) he strolled around the vehicle eyeing everything up. Stopping at the rear door he motioned us over and said "Interno, interno" which we took to mean he wanted to see inside. Inside was a little unkempt due to Annie not having dusted or hoovered that day, so it all looked a little untidy. However, he stuck his head inside, let out a long sigh, re-emerged and with a condescending wave of his hand he said "Go, go" and walked away. Entente cordial, I think not. I drove away down the looping valley road in the evening light towards Cuneo. Somewhere down the line I took a wrong turn onto a road that eventually came to a scruffy village in the hills where it changed to a dusty track between rows of ramshackle houses. In the twilight people were gathered in groups outside doorways while some ragged children chased chickens, and everyone stared. Nobody moved, nobody waved and nobody spoke. They just stared at us in a creepy kind of way as I confidently drove past on a road as it turned out to nowhere. A hundred yards or so after the last house the track finished by the edge of a dark wood which was a bit embarrassing to say the least as we would now, shamefacedly have to run the gauntlet back through the village of the damned. I looked in the rear view mirror and could see what seemed to be the entire village still staring at us. I decided that this wood was where they were going to murder the pair of us and no one would ever know. At least I had clean underpants on that day, which I consider to be quite important if one is going to be murdered as it would not do to depart this world in soiled underpants. It is a very British sort of thing. Annie was of a similar opinion (not about my underpants, but about being murdered) so I turned the vehicle around and drove back past all the villagers who still continued to gape at us, but at least we emerged the other side somewhat relieved and definitely not murdered. It had been a strangely discomforting experience, but after several miles and in near darkness we pulled into an overgrown lane to sleep for the night. Six o'clock the next morning we did not wake up to the twittering of birds but to the sound of people pushing with some difficulty between the sides of the Land Rover and the hedges on either side. I know they were experiencing some problems because they kept thumping the sides and yelling 'Stupido Inglese' and 'Inglese Bastardi' and something about 'Blocca la strada' none of which required interpretation from our phrase book. All went quiet after ten minutes so we sheepishly crept outside to discover a factory just down the road and we had parked in a lane which was obviously a worker's short-cut from somewhere. This had not been a good choice and would not be going down on our list of top ten favourite overnight stays.

In the days that followed we visited all the usual tourist sites. We leaned against the Leaning Tower of Pisa, went to the Coliseum in Rome, although there was no entertainment that afternoon as it was the gladiators half day and it seems you just cannot get the Christians any more. Not like the good old days when they were ten a penny and always up for a bit of savage animal wrestling or providing additional lighting by becoming a flaming torch stuck on a pole. In those far off days they were real crowd pullers. Those Christians knew how to lay on a good show, albeit unwillingly. We visited the Pantheon, the Trevi fountains and the remains of the Roman Forum which at one point was over-run by scores of manky moggies. These cats not only looked a health threat but also stalked us along the top of the walls and I felt it was going to be only a matter of time before I would be wearing one as a Davy Crockett hat with its claws clamped firmly into my head. A heady mixture of heat and cat pee made for an arresting experience. The following day we walked through the deserted streets of Pompeii, deserted that is, apart from two American tourists who asked 'How did they let it get into such a dilapidated state?' We arrived in Naples in the evening and I drove up a narrow street that smelt like an open sewer because in reality it was an open sewer. Skin and bones ragamuffin children hung onto the back of the Land Rover as I careered along the street with people shouting and waving at us, but again they were not saying how pleased they were to see us and hoped we were having a wonderful time in their wonderful country. Far from it, because what they were trying to tell us was that we were going the wrong way up a one-way street. In due course we escaped the claustrophobic confines of 'See Naples and Die' a phrase coined when Naples was alleged to be one of the most beautiful cities in the world. Whoever first uttered those words had obviously not been up that one-way street where I had just driven along, although on reflection perhaps there was an aptness about the phrase as the street was so objectionable and smelly that if one was to linger too long then one might indeed 'See Naples and Die' of dysentery or something equally as ghastly. From here we headed due south into quite open and barren terrain, yet despite the apparent lack of human habitation a cesspit aroma seemed to be following us and it was getting to the stage where

Annie and I were beginning to surreptitiously eye each other suspecting that one of us was having a chronic bout of diarrhoea and had messed their pants but was not owning up! This turned out not to be the case and the pong remained a mystery.

Somewhere in the Appenine mountains (possibly lost but I'm not owning up to it) I took a side road looking for a place to spend the night. The road climbed steeply for some miles before petering out onto a bare earth plateau. We got out of the Land Rover and looked about us for a way forward. It was deathly quiet in the evening sunlight and any signs of a track did not seem to exist. I decided to drive across to the far side where there was a treeline that would at least afford some degree of shelter. We passed a post with half a sign on it saying 'Mina' which we took to mean that we were in a mining area. About half a mile further on I jumped on the brakes alongside another sign on a post which this time was complete with the words 'Mina de Terra', and so as not to leave the unfortunate reader in any doubt (no phrase book needed here) there was an illustration beneath of an exploding bomb. "Oh! B......s I shouted. "We're in the middle of a b....y mine field!" Annie immediately stuck her head out of the window and starting looking for menacing lumps in the ground that might be hiding a bomb. At least we now knew what that dilapidated sign meant lying in a hedge way back along the road saying 'Zona Militare.' The only option open to us that might hopefully ensure that both of us did not cause a very loud bang and become part of the landscape was to carefully and laboriously reverse along our own tyre tracks, which was precisely what I did. Having successfully completed this challenge and eventually got my head back the right way round I saw a track leading into some scrubby bushes that would conceal us nicely for the night. I reversed in and we had supper beneath the stars.

The following morning we lay in bed listening to the not very distant sound of rifle and machine gun fire. Neither of us actually cared anymore and despite the risk that at any minute a hail of bullets might come whistling through the bushes and riddle the Land Rover, thus turning it into a well-ventilated heap of scrap metal, we sat outside and had breakfast. The gunfire was now getting quite close and we could clearly hear men shouting 'Avanti! Avanti! and 'Attacco!' which seem fairly self-explanatory. Regardless of the war that seemed to have erupted around us we had breakfast, packed everything up and prepared ourselves for the dash from our cover. I revved the engine and gunned out of the thicket where we found ourselves confronted by a number of soldiers scurrying about with small bushes stuck on their helmets, wielding rifles and pistols. Another soldier close by had a large radio strapped on his back and was yattering ninety to the dozen into the mouthpiece, probably placing an order for two dozen pizzas, and elsewhere bushy helmets appeared above dug-outs. Abruptly everything came to a halt as we emerged unexpectedly onto their battle ground and roared past in a cloud of dust. Somewhat taken aback by the sight of us, we were almost out of earshot before a torrent of abuse was aimed at us with clenched fists along the usual format of "Crazy Inglese! Stupido Inglese! In fact all the things we were now getting used to. The main thing is we escaped unscathed and made it back to the road and spent most of that day driving through land that was fenced off and had signs stating that this whole area was 'Zona Militare' so, no surprise there then. I think it safe to say we had well and truly got the message and that night we decided to play safe.

Playing safe was arriving in the dark at a proper international campsite with all the necessary facilities that made it home from home. The man at reception welcomed us, took our passports, relieved us of some Liras and in pidgin English gave us directions through the main site to a quiet pitch beyond some trees which we could have all to ourselves. The campsite bar was alive with happy holidaymakers knocking back bottles of vino and having a jolly time. Unwittingly we soon put a stop to that for as I drove among the tents I was unable to see the overhead electricity cable that had been slung between the branches of a couple of trees. I felt a slight tug and heard a kind of pinging noise as the cable caught on the cap of a jerry can and snapped followed by an awful lot of lights going out all over the site. We gulped and carried on to the dark cover of the trees hoping that no one had seen us, which as luck would have it, nobody did. On reflection it was fortunate that the jerry can lid had been a tight fit as a combination of an electrical spark and petrol fumes could have resulted in an explosion of pyroclastic proportions that would certainly have illuminated the campsite! A couple of hours later after we had eaten and gone to bed we assumed the bar was closing for the night as there were the sounds of cheery Italians echoing around the site which were suddenly replaced by the sounds of highly irritated Italians discovering they were without lights in their tents. Amid the shouting of 'Non si accende!' (no lights) and 'Torcia, una torcia!' came the roar of car engines being fired up shining headlamps into tents. In short there was pandemonium and we lying unaffected in our bed were the unseen culprits. They were not happy bunnies. However, it would appear we were not going to get completely let off the hook for there was a price to pay. Payback time came around three thirty in the morning when I felt something crawl over my shoulder and something else on my chest, and my stomach, and my legs, in fact it felt as if there were many things sharing the sleeping bag. I woke Annie who only got part way through asking me why I had woken her when she quickly realised that she was sharing the sleeping bag with more than just me. I switched on the light to reveal ants, lots of ants crawling all over us, but even more disconcerting was when I looked beneath the bed and saw a thick column of them marching under the rear door and raiding the food locker. We were forced to get out of bed and out of the vehicle. Once outside I found that a single blade of grass touching the mud flap had been enough to give the ants a free pass to a feast at our expense and they were busily engaged infiltrating an open bag of sugar. "God! The little s…s are everywhere." I raged. "We'll have to empty all the b….y lockers!" A sleepy Annie muttered something about divine justice and as the rest of the campsite slept peacefully through the night we set about emptying the food lockers and our clothes lockers cursing and mass murdering ants in the process. Everything had to be wiped and shaken before piling it all elsewhere as we emptied out the back of the Land Rover. Now guess who was not a happy bunny? These ants had been determined and apart from the problem they would have encountered in getting us out under the rear door I feel sure they would have carried the pair of us away as we slept in our sleeping bag only for us to later wake up deep inside the claustrophobic confines of an ant hill. This would not have been a good start to the day. As it turned out the day started extremely early for by the time we had evicted or annihilated the unwelcome intruders it was getting light, so we knocked up the site manager, retrieved our passports and beat a hasty retreat before last night's bedlam was traced to us.

The following night we reached Taranto which is a busy port with squalid back streets where young guttersnipes aged between eight to ten years tried annoyingly hard to sell us boxes of two hundred cigarettes which they had somehow acquired from the ships. I drove away from the town and came across an abandoned bauxite quarry, which despite the rock faces glowing a spooky white in the moonlight did have the advantage of being secluded, quiet and ant free. We were driven from our bed early the next day by searing heat and decided to spend a day at a beach. Around lunchtime we parked on a headland overlooking a beach that was strewn with peculiar soft, hairy balls of varying sizes which I presumed were some sort of sea plant. As we frolicked about in the warm embracing water we noticed up on the headland a kid on a moped who seemed to be very intently watching us. Upon our return to the Land Rover we quickly realised that he had been the lookout for his mates who had smashed the passenger side window and opened the door from inside. It seemed they were probably a bunch of half-wits as the only things stolen were some small change and a sheaf knife I had owned since a boy. I must have been about twelve years old when my father, bought it for me from Stones the ironmongers at the bottom of Green Lane in Derby for our first ever camping weekend. I used to strut about with it hanging from my belt as in those days anyone could walk about armed to the teeth with knives and nobody gave a fig, and neither did anyone feel they were going to be stabbed to death at the drop of a hat. Anyway, we needed to make an insurance claim for the damage, so out came the Italian phrase book to look up the words for a police station. "Stazione polizia?" I enquired of the first man we came across. "No polizia!" he shouted and ran away. What strange behaviour we thought and tried someone else who was just getting into his car. "Stazione polizia?" I asked again. "No, no polizia!" he replied somewhat agitated and leapt into his car and drove off. Talk about there is never a policeman around when you want one. "Do you think they're all members of the Mafia?" I asked Annie. "I'm sick of all this stupid carry on" she announced. "I'm going to find a telephone" and she stomped off in a very determined manner to a hotel across the road. The outcome from all this is that she stormed in, and into the middle of a wedding reception, grabbed a waiter and asked for a telephone.

"Telephono per favour?" she demanded in her best phrase book Italian.

"Telephono?" replied the waiter.

"Yes, telephono, emergenza" she continued, trying hard not to lose her rag with him.

"Ah!" he exclaimed and taking her by the arm pushed her into a tight cubbyhole beneath some stairs where there was a telephone.

"Gracias" she replied.

"You Eengleesh, yes?" he asked.

"Yes, I need the police".

"Ah, yes, polizia not good. I reeing for you" he said, leering at her and no doubt thinking that being squashed under the stairs with a young, long blonde-haired girl was preferable to waiting on the rowdy guests. Annie managed to convey to him that the car had been broken into, so the waiter then launched into an excited ten minute shouting match with whoever was on the other end of the phone. A couple of wedding guests wandered over to see what all the fuss was about, but he just waved them away. He finally slammed the phone down and told Annie that she would have to go to the police station as they were not going to come to her. This was beginning to have that 'déjà vu' feel about it as she explained to the waiter that she had been down that route already but nobody wanted go anywhere near the police station. At this point he rushed outside, flagged down the first motorist that came along and apparently ordered this bewildered individual to show us the way. We jumped back into the Land Rover and set off following the man in the car. After a short distance the man stuck his arm out of the window, pointed to a building across the road and fled the scene at great speed. Was everybody around here a criminal wanted by the police? With reservations we entered the building and were shown into an office where two policemen were loafing about smoking and reading newspapers. We attempted between us to explain to these two reprobates what had happened. Sadly only one of them spoke some pidgin English.

"Our car was broken into" I began.

"Ah! Auto rubata? Robbed?" he questioned.

"Yes. I need signed insurance papers, documents" I answered. There then followed a lengthy interrogation as to where it had taken place and where were we staying; and to add to the growing confusion one of the policemen produced a battered map which he proceeded to unfold very carefully and very slowly as if it was the Turin Shroud he was handling. We pointed out on the map where we were robbed, but he insisted on asking us where we had camped which we did not want to tell him as we thought staying in an unused quarry might be imprudent. "Dove hai camp?" he continued, prodding the map with his nicotine stained finger. "Where you camp?." We told him we were passing through on our way to catch the ferry at Brindisi. After several attempts he gave up. By now the other policeman had embarked upon spending the longest time that anyone in the entire world has ever spent on folding up a map. As he got underway with his folding and to the background noise of rustling paper the other policeman launched into a ludicrous and time wasting conversation.

"Si mangia yoghurt?" he enquired. "Breakfast yes?"

"What?" I answered, not really having a clue what he was talking about beyond the words yoghurt and breakfast.

"Yoghurt" he replied. "You eeet yogurt?"

"No, I don't eat yoghurt".

"You eeet yoghurt, breakfast, si?" he continued, staring at me.

"No, I not eat yoghurt for breakfast". In the background the other policeman continued to wrestle with the map first folding it and then unfolding it accompanied by a lot of grunting. Our interrogator then turned on Annie.

"You eeet yoghurt"

"No" she answered.

"You no eeet yoghurt? Isz good yoghurt, si" he said patting a stomach that looked eight months pregnant. "I eeet yogurt, si, good yoghurt".

By now I was beginning to think that either he had shares in a yoghurt factory or else he was completely mad. I was more inclined to think the latter. The map folding saga continued among sighs and grunts of impending frustration.

"Firmare documenti, please" I begged him as time ticked by.

"Ah, yes, documenti" he muttered and scratched his head. He paused meditatively for a second or so, then leaning forward on the table he fixed us both with a perplexing gaze and said "Why not you eeet yogurt?" My thoughts turned to murder. I wanted to drown him in a giant tub of yoghurt. In fact I wanted to pulverize him into yoghurt. There followed a sort of silent stand-off until he turned and left the room returning some time later with the signed documents. In his absence the other policeman with the map suddenly stood up, wiped his brow, lit a cigarette and looked at the crumpled map on his table. Then like a petulant school boy he threw it on the floor, kicked it under the table and went to gaze out of the window. For our part we had wasted the best of two hours and were close to the brink of insanity ourselves before we were finally able to leave the police station. We were rather baffled by the fact that neither policeman had actually stepped outside to see what damage had been done to our vehicle. I guess it was all too much of an effort. We spent that night back in the quarry mentally drained and having nightmares about policemen dressed as pots of yoghurt!

In the morning I awoke with a badly blocked ear and a sound like rushing water inside my head. It was extremely irritating and I just had to find a chemist shop. I drove to a small town, found a 'farmaceutico' and we boldly walked in.

"Beunos dias" I said "Non parlo Italiano".

"I don't speak English" replied the man behind the counter which confused me because he just had, and how did he know we were English?" The only two words from our notoriously useless phrase book was 'orrechio' meaning ear and 'congestione' which apparently referred to a traffic jam, so armed with these two words I announced to him that I had a traffic jam in my ear. Not surprisingly this amused him. I stuck a finger in my ear to suggest a blockage whereupon he said "Nuoto in mare?"

"In mare" I echoed, wondering what a horse had to do with my complaint. Annie was quickly on the case saying "He means the sea you numbskull, like 'mer' French for sea" (she could speak French quite well, show-off) and of course she was right for the chemist was shouting "Mare! Mare! and pretending to swim breast stroke across the shop.

"Ah! Si, si" I replied enthusiastically and joined him in the front crawl around the shop as I had never mastered breast stroke. Outside a small crowd had gathered. Some peered through the shop window and others gingerly hovered in the doorway watching the pair of us swimming alongside the counter. Next he produced a small bottle of liquid that looked not unlike urine which if that was the case then I could provide my own. There would still be the small matter of mastering the art of peeing into my own ear, but I felt sure that time and patience would win the day. Next he waved his arms about pointing at the sun and then at the bottle. This had me completely flummoxed but the crowd thought it highly entertaining. Finally we got the message that the bottle had to be warmed in the sun before use. As we left the shop we received a cheer from the crowd along with some half-hearted clapping, so I responded with a quick bow before driving away. We had now missed the Brindisi ferry. Both of us seemed to be suffering from fatigue and try as we might we could not get a replacement side window anywhere and consequently, in the interest of security we could only leave the vehicle provided I could find a high wall to park it against so nobody could put an arm through to open the door. This became pretty tiresome so we decided to head up the eastern highway to Bologna which we did in a single day. I use the word we, because Annie took over the driving for part of the way and I have to say she did very well considering she had only ever had a few lessons and never taken her driving test. We did get away with it, illegal though it was. We wandered around Europe for a few weeks still unable to get a new window, until the parking became not only challenging but annoyingly ridiculous, so in the finish we caught an overnight ferry back to Dover. Our first port of call was a visit to a doctor as neither of us felt too well. We were put in isolation at a friend's house because we were suspected of having Hepatitis, gastroenteritis, dropsy or some such sickness and told not to go anywhere until the doctor had the results of our tests. I do not suppose it would have happened if we had eaten yogurt for breakfast. We finally got the all-clear, were given some tablets to take which for all we knew might well have been Bob Martin Conditioning tablets and were sent on our way back to Derby and familiar territory.

The Last Post

The big question now was what were we going to do with ourselves as we had nowhere to live, no jobs, no income and rapidly diminishing funds? We tried hard to look on the bright only to find there was no bright side. Sometime later we were offered the cottage near Taddington and on a misty day in mid-autumn I opened the cottage door to be greeted once more by the familiar smell of damp mustiness and leaking gas. Everything looked drab, dank and unwelcoming, but we had to make the best of it and once the fire was alight and the kettle boiling it became a bit more appealing. We spent a couple of weeks simply enjoying the dales and the company of a hitch-hiker we picked up who was an American and liked a pipe of Voortrekker tobacco, which in itself was sufficient grounds to forge a friendship. He was travelling around Europe and came back a year later in time to be my best man when Annie and I tied the knot. Evenings were spent either in the pub or more often than not sitting huddled close to the fire listening to an ancient transistor radio belting out pop songs. There seemed to be a lot of opportunities for us to join in with Elton John singing *Goodbye Yellow Brick Road* and *Goodbye Norma Jean* and make as much racket as we liked for there were no near neighbours to upset. As time wore on it became increasingly evident that we needed some kind of income. The farmer who owned the cottage thought he could give us a job to do on his farm. Now as farmers go he was not noted for being hearty, jovial, fun loving and a laugh a minute. He was more the miserable, truculent, accusative and suspicious of everything and everybody type. Be that as it may, he offered us a job of painting a barn roof in National Park green, but only, I suspect because he did not want to do it himself on account of the barn being extremely high with an ageing asbestos roof which was an absolute death trap. It would have been very easy to have slipped off, crashed to the ground and sustained some ghastly crippling injuries that would be compounded by falling into a bed of viscious nettles surrounding the barn, or being spiked on some fiendish piece of farm machinery of which there was plenty lying about. Alternatively, there was a fair chance that the roof could give way beneath our weight and send us plummeting through the air and again crashing to the ground inside the barn sustaining ghastly injuries (this time without the added bonus of stinging nettles) and again be punctured on another piece of evil-looking machinery. We really were spoilt for choice! Weighing up the odds it was not a job either of us fancied, but with barely more than half a dozen eggs and two oatcakes left in the larder we agreed to do it. First we had to lug numerous ten litre tins of paint up onto the roof by means of a rickety old wooden ladder that I assumed had been left over from the boarding arrangements of Noah's Ark. It bowed and creaked in a very alarming manner and did nothing to inspire confidence. Stingy farmer 'Grumpy' only paid us a miserly sum for which we risked life and limb labouring in the cold wind slopping green paint onto a roof that seemed endless, not to mention the painfully bruised knees we suffered from kneeling on the corrugations. To our relief we completed the task without any mishaps, but it had really been a case of needs must. The harsh reality was that we needed a rather more sustainable income. Painting barn roofs was never going to be a paying or challenging career, unless you were an utter moron who had never done anything more exciting in your life than hurtle downhill on a bicycle without holding onto the handlebars.

Annie thought she might like to work in caring for the elderly and applied for a position at a residential home in Bakewell where she was accepted. This required me to drive her in every morning and collect her again at the end of her shift. The thing is that farmer 'Grumpy' had got a tad testy and banned me from driving across the two fields that separated the cottage from a lane because my Land Rover was making an untidy track across his grass. In the dark, bleak mornings of oncoming winter we had to be up at six thirty ready to meet the first challenge of the day which was to light the oil lamp beside the bed (for bed read sunken damp mattress on a tired, sunken wire-mesh base) which necessitated rolling back a corner of the mattress to strike a match on the iron frame as this was the only damp-free surface available. Under normal circumstances I might concede to this being a risky procedure that could easily result in the mattress catching light, us finding ourselves homeless and farmer 'Grumpy' having a blood vessel-bursting strop. Because everything was permanently damp the chances of this happening were about as remote as me winning the Nobel Prize for an outstanding contribution to quantum electrodynamics! (Of course I know what it means I looked it up in a dictionary). After a cup of tea we would set out across the two fields in complete darkness hoping not to step on, or fall over a slumbering cow then drive to Bakewell. After only a week of this a senior member of staff at the home asked Annie why she always came to work with cow muck plastered on the soles of her shoes, presumably because it contravened health regulations or maybe she was just curious. When Annie explained that in order to get to work she had to cross two fields in pitch darkness and was unable to sometimes spot the lurking cow pats as they did not glow in the dark or give off a warning siren when she got close to one, she was told to go and buy a pair of wellington boots and a torch. There always has to be some smarty pants with a ready answer.

After several weeks of living in rustic isolation my parents said we could move in with them temporarily because they knew of a flat in Derby that was shortly to be available and we could find work more easily in the city. The bad news was that the flat was not available until the New Year and my parents were going away for Christmas, and I got a distinct impression that they did not want us in the house until they returned. Now whether or not this had anything to do with my mother once being suspicious of us abusing her Baby Burco clothes drying drum is questionable. The thing is we were only drying off some laundry. The Baby Burco was part of my mother's laundry equipment to modernise her washdays. She was of the old school when washday, always a Monday would see her boiling large pans of handkerchiefs, pants and knickers on the cooker top filling the kitchen with clouds of steam and an odd 'I can't quite put my finger on it' smell. In the centre of the floor would be the corrugated-sided galvanised dolly tub which contained the rest of the clothes that she would pound energetically with a copper-headed posser (a wooden pole with a sort of upturned colander on the end) accompanied by gurgling, squelching and spurting noises more associated with someone suffering from a chronic bowel disorder than anything as hygienic as washing clothes. After laboriously winding everything through an ancient mangle, she would hang all the clothes outside on the garden line. In winter the bed-sheets often resembled large sheets of stiff white card as they hung frozen from the line. All that was now history as the Baby Burco dryer and a Hoovermatic top loading Twin Tub rescued her from the Dark Ages and washdays changed forever. This electric drying device resembled an oil drum with a smaller one inside that whizzed round at frightening speed and for this reason alone (as we were to discover) is why it should not be operated on a smooth surface like a Formica kitchen top. Take it from me once it gets underway and reaches maximum speed then you will be quickly convinced that very shortly this noisy, whirring, vibrating gadget is destined to launch itself into outer space, or in our case off the kitchen top and into the air to land badly on the floor. Not surprisingly the lid flew open and we ducked and dived as a tornado of soggy socks, knickers, trousers and shirts flew around the kitchen in all directions. The thing only ground to a halt because the plug had been yanked out of the wall socket and for a time flailed about in the air threatening to cut us off at the knees like the whirling blade on a Roman chariot before everything finally went quiet, at which point we presumed it was dead. We approached it with caution just in case it was only playing dead and might unexpectedly spring back to life when we were close enough for it to take revenge on us. Apart from a small chip missing from the plug it survived pretty well and much too our utter amazement and relief was still in working order. The designer had obviously considered all eventualities even idiots like us who might use it anywhere except the most sensible of places like a floor. Still, there was no harm done and when my mother returned from her twice weekly shop having just lugged bags full of food up from the bus stop all seemed well.

"Phew!" she gasped. "Put the kettle on I'm propa' parched, and what's more I had to sit next to that Mrs Jones woman on the bus."

"Who's Mrs Jones?" I answered.

"You know. Her son Rodney fancied your sister in junior school, but I'm sure she hardly ever washes herself. I thought to myself, ruddy 'eck what a pong and I had to sit next to her as the bus was full."

"Oh right, that Mrs Jones" I replied.

"I was glad when she got off at the top of Derwent Street. Phew, what a pong" insisted my mother twitching her nose at the same time. My mother was very astute when it came to detecting 'pongs' and probably missed out on a career with the police force as a human sniffer dog. She was also very 'eagle-eyed' and never seemed to miss anything and would doggedly search in the manner of a manhunt for a serial killer if, for example, she reached for a tin of sardines in the larder and discovered the key to roll back the lid had come off and was nowhere to be found. No stone was left unturned and everyone was a suspect until the missing sardine key had been located. The outcome to all this was that her 'eagle eyes' spotted the missing fragment of white plastic plug on the floor. "What's this? It looks like a bit off a plug. Now where would that have come from?"

"No idea" we said in unison. Shall we put the kettle on?" She was rapidly led away from further investigation by the lure of a cup of tea. My mother's general philosophy when it came to drinking, especially tea was 'if it's wet and warm I'll drink it.' I wonder if this doctrine of hers would have stood the test had she suddenly found herself cast adrift at sea for several days in a life-raft and the only prospect of a 'wet and warm' drink being from filtering her own urine through an old stocking. It was merely a passing thought. A day later she found a damp pair of my underpants behind the fridge, but her initial inquiry simply met with a couple of blank faces. I still think she had her suspicions that leaned heavily in our direction, but either way we were out on the streets and the true spirit of Christmas prevailed by there being, quite literally, no room at the inn.

There was obviously not going to be a full blow-out Christmas dinner for us and we had to make do with the only place we could find open which happened to be an Indian take-away. The menu meant nothing to me as I had never eaten anything Indian and even Annie was only a few curries in front of me. We blindly ordered a couple of meals and retired to the Land Rover with a plastic tray each viewing the steaming concoction with some misgivings. There seemed to be lumps of greyish meat attached to a bony shape that looked not unlike the skull of a cat floating in some kind of spicy vegetable slop. If it was the head of a decapitated cat then it evidently had a mate whose severed head was in Annie's tray. It was a real appetite killer and events like this linger long in the mind and quickly come to the forefront when you find yourself in a similar set of circumstances as I did many years later while out one evening with friends in Portugal. We were in a crowded back-street restaurant much frequented by the locals and presented with a menu which stretched well beyond our meagre knowledge of the language until we spotted the word 'porco' which was self-explanatory. Thoughts turned to a nice pork chop, or chump steak with some tasty fat despite not understanding the word 'coracao' which preceded it. What we got has since been likened to the equivalent of 'slave food' and consisted of a bowl of sludgy, grey boiled rice out of which reared lumps of grey meat that was identified as pig's heart. It was like chewing on a tennis ball with a flavour I have yet to find words that come anywhere close to describing and with a consistency similar I imagine, to a hard-boiled scrotum. I would never want to experience that taste or texture ever again, so if ever I eat out anywhere I always diligently scan the menu in case hard-boiled scrotum is listed. The locals, however, were tucking into platefuls of the stuff, talking and laughing, obviously in good spirits. We, on the other hand, sat beneath a cloud of gloom our energies being spent on laborious half-hearted (no pun intended) chewing until we finally gave up and left with our appetites sadly wanting and our stomachs in shock.

Anyway, back in Derby having survived Christmas it was now early January and Annie and I moved into an upstairs flat off Burton Road. I joined the Post Office and Annie joined Kingsway Psychiatric Hospital as a trainee nurse, and shortly afterwards we were joined by a long-haired Alsatian bitch who went by the name of Mundy, or sometimes Mundy Scruffer which had nothing whatsoever to do with her appearance for she was most definitely not untidy, scruffy or scro(u)fulous. As flats go it was spacious enough for two people and had a spare bedroom, not that we had anyone spare to put in it. We were able to keep the place very warm during the winter owing to the fact that the long-term tenant downstairs had the task of periodically emptying our gas meter. Fortunately for us she had lost the key for the padlock thus allowing us to leave a meagre amount in the meter box when she called while re-circulating a one pound coin umpteen times. She never took a reading and no one ever complained of a discrepancy, so naturally we found the whole thing very economically acceptable. We had more than a few run-ins with 'her' downstairs because she slept in the room beneath our bedroom and was forever complaining about the noise we were allegedly making at night. We thought this was more than a little petty minded of her especially as it was not every night of the week we had athletic sex, leaping from the top of the wardrobe shouting 'Geronimo', or swinging from the light fitting and mimicking ape noises, before crashing onto the bed and using it as a trampoline followed by a climactic 'coup de grace'. Perhaps living for years alone had soured her sense of fun, or maybe she was simply an erotophobiac. She even complained that I made too much noise descending the stairs early in the morning and slamming the front door on my way out to work. Not having mastered a technique of descending stairs without touching any of the treads left me with an unsolvable problem, whereas the supposed door slamming could easily have been remedied by removing it from its hinges and doing away with a front door altogether. When I suggested this to her she failed to see the funny side and merely looked at me with blank eyes accompanied by a slight creasing of her lips. I could clearly see why there was nobody sharing her bed to take her mind of the trivialities of life. However, I was not the only person disturbing the quiet of the night for once a week in the summer a woman living opposite would emerge after midnight and methodically embark upon clipping the privet hedge in front of her house apparently oblivious of the time of day. It is not as if she went in for anything fancy like a line of prancing peacocks, or a manicured leafy depiction of Leonardo's 'The Last Supper' to surprise us all with in the morning when we gazed awestruck from the bedroom window. It was just a flat, lineal-edged privet hedge created by the light of a street lamp with a pair of clippers unimaginatively wielded by either a she-vampire, or the use of night vision goggles. I imagine she was eventually taken away for her own good.

My initiation into Post Office life entailed a farcical three-day course on how to be a post man, deal with the public and sign the Official Secrets Act as I was now working for the Queen, not that she was personally paying my wages or ever turned up to see how I was getting on. I thought I once spotted her boarding a bus in Midland Road, but I guess I was mistaken. My first real day of being a 'postie' saw me being shown how to sort the mail into streets and house numbers before I was bundled into the back of a van with a chap who was going to guide me round my first 'walk'. Fifteen minutes later we were evicted from the back of the van along with our mail bags into a dimly lit street heavens knows where in search of front doors and letter boxes. It was fairly straight forward stuff and my colleague launched into the hitherto unknown delights of tramping the streets in the early morning. "See No.14?" he started. "She always gets dressed in front of the window and always has the curtains open." And sure enough, there at the window of No.14 was a slim woman in a chic little black number about to disrobe and put on her underwear. He continued throughout the 'walk' with No.36 who had big breasts, No.115 who sticks her rear end up in the air in front of the window as she performs her early morning work-out, and of course Flat 1A with a ground floor bathroom window that is always sufficiently ajar to be able to peek in as you pass and presumably be suitably distracted as you fumble in the dark trying to push something into her letterbox. The most notable address I was told was that of a certain lady at No.69, who had a lot of Recorded Deliveries that required a signature. My colleague refused to comment further on the matter and said that sometime in the near future I would find out for myself.

Being a newcomer I was given a variety of shifts so as to be able to try my hand at all things postal and thereby be of maximum use. Sometimes I would be out early mornings doing a 'walk' and another time I would be sorting mail through the night. I was soon given a nickname because I had a large beard and wore the popular Spanish Fell boots which meant that no one could hear me approaching, so I was often referred to as 'Creeping Jesus' which as nicknames go was not too unflattering. The constant change of shifts played havoc with my digestive system which never knew what time of day it was supposed to be, as one week I would be on nights gorging on steak and kidney pie followed by steamed treacle pudding and custard at two thirty in the morning, while the next week I would be starting at five in the morning whereupon my eating habits would change accordingly. I once had to work all Sunday afternoon and early evening doing nothing but hang around the loading bay waiting for one delivery of mail from the train station and that was it. For the rest of the time there was absolutely nothing to do but play security guard in case someone came to furtively steal a mail trolley as that is all there was available. This was not rocket science, but at double time it was good for my wage packet at the end of the week! The weeks drifted by and on the home front 'her' downstairs continued to complain about me slamming the front door at four thirty in the morning on my way out and in return, I complained about her radio being on too loud when I was trying to sleep during the day when I was on night shift. She then complained about me slamming the front door when I came in off night shift at six o'clock in the morning and I complained about her continually complaining. As you will have gathered life was far from harmonious and I sometimes wished that Mundy the dog would one day pounce on her and eat her so she could complain no more, although I suspect she would probably still complain about Mundy making too much noise as she crunched her way through some of the bony bits.

Predictably, the day dawned when I had to stand in for a 'postie' who had gone away on holiday and had been doing my original round, and equally predictable among my deliveries was a Recorded Delivery for No.69, which of course, required a signature. Now the mystery, if indeed there was one, would finally be unveiled and I marched up the garden path like a man on a mission. I noticed the bedroom light was on as I knocked on the door. "Just a minute" a voice trilled from somewhere beyond the door. It was a lot less than a minute when the door was flung open wide and there she stood, a sight for sore eyes in pink, smiling like the Cheshire cat and pretending to be coy. I got the distinct feeling she had been waiting behind the door ready for this moment.

"Oh, my goodness!" she tittered. "You've caught me on the hop. I haven't even put my dressing gown on" she exclaimed, which of course was self-evident. She was about mid-forties, substantial in all areas especially her bosom which loomed, vast and voluminous in the extreme and jiggled like two enormous gelatinous jellies beneath her very short, very plunging see-through pink negligee. The expression 'She would have no trouble floating on her back' passed through my mind as I took in the rest of the vision standing in the doorway. Her thighs were sufficiently hefty to crack coconuts between, while her knees and lower legs were sufficiently sturdy to have graced and supported any heavy kitchen table had she another matching pair tucked away somewhere! Her feet were hidden by a pair of exceedingly furry slippers that gave the impression she was standing on two dead pink cats. This expansive spectacle in pink that threatened to flop out in all directions was otherwise near naked and strangely surreal.

"You must have brought me something special" she giggled, clasping her hands to her chest in mock excitement and rubbing her legs together like a sexually aroused grasshopper.

"Yes, I have" I blurted out through a sudden fit of coughing.

"My, that's a nasty cough you have. I've got something I could rub on your chest" she crooned flirtatiously. In actual fact she had moved so close to me that she was almost rubbing a couple of things on my chest anyway, so I am not too sure what else she had in mind.

"I have a Recorded Delivery that needs signing for" I replied fumbling in my top pocket for a pencil and the recording book.

"Ooooh!" she cooed, "a pencil. I hope you've got plenty of lead in it?" she giggled as I handed her the book and pencil. The two gigantic breasts gyrated inside her flimsy pink negligee as if they were fighting with each other in an attempt to burst out and engulf me.

"Ooooh!" she started off again. "Look at me, I'm all fingers and thumbs this morning" as she clumsily dropped the pencil down inside her enveloping cleavage. "There's no telling where it's got to now" she continued as she tried to tug the low slung neckline down in an effort to see the pencil. "Can you see it anywhere?" she asked coyly while pushing her décolletage towards my face which I have to admit held me temporarily spellbound.

"Actually, I can."

"Hmmm, well if you want to get it out then I don't mind. I still can't see it" she crooned once more, pawing her breasts in anticipation of me taking up the offer.

"That's no problem" I announced boldly as I stooped down to pick up the pencil which I noted had fallen past the two intimidating barriers and landed between the two dead, pink cats. As I retrieved it off the floor she moved forward slightly as though hoping to catch my head with her negligee on my way up, but luckily for me it was far too short, so I narrowly escaped being caught in a pink net and floundering in wanton flesh, like a gasping herring being hauled up in the net of a deep sea trawler. She turned to hold the book against the doorframe to sign her name while at the same time purposely thrusting out her buttocks in such a manner that I clearly remember having a fleeting image in my mind's eye of someone frantically beating a pair of bongo drums. I handed her the package and she put the book and pencil back in my top pocket unashamedly patting me hard with the flat of her hand saying, "There we are, we wouldn't want your pencil coming out would we, at least not until you're ready to use it?" The front door then slammed shut as she disappeared behind it and I made my way back down the garden path somewhat bemused by the whole experience. Shortly after this I was overcome with an irrepressible desire to sink my teeth into a bacon-butty. It is a great comfort to know that one's sub-conscious will always deliver a suitable antidote. Later that day when I was relating to Annie what had happened earlier on in the darkness before dawn it seemed too phantasmagorical to have been of this world and I began to think that somehow I had been temporarily transferred to a parallel universe where No.69 was for real! I never had occasion to do that 'walk' again so some things are best left in the past and abandoned to the dark recesses of the mind.

While I was posting letters and trying to avoid doorstep confrontations with sex-crazed women, Annie was meeting challenges of her own as she joined the rest of the staff at Kingsway at seven o'clock in the morning only to find herself in a warzone of noise, mayhem and chaos. Whenever she walked through the doors into the ward it was as if all hell had broken loose as patients screamed at each other and threw anything they could get their hands on across the room or at each other. It turned out to be fortunate that I was able to collect her from work because of what frequently happened to her during the course of a shift. More often than not I would see her walking towards me where I was parked wearing her three-quarter length coat and carrying a plastic bag containing her uniform and sometimes her underwear. Had she kept a diary of events then a typical week would read something along these lines.

Monday. A patient threw a mug of tea over me.

Tuesday. A patient piddled up the front of me.

Wednesday. A patient vomited over me.

Thursday. A patient ripped my tunic and wiped food down the front.

Friday. A patient set fire to his mattress and the hem of my tunic got scorched.

Saturday. Yippee, two days off. I might spend today having a nervous breakdown.

Sunday. Oh God! Have I really got to go to that madhouse again in the morning?!

Annie spent the best part of a year at the Kingsway Psychiatric Hospital before deciding this was not going to be her choice of career as she reckoned that too much exposure to all this might see her swopping her torn, soiled and abused tunic for one of those specially designed jackets with straps and buckles that tighten behind the back.

Generally, our time from work was spent travelling about in the Land Rover which had the basic necessities of a collapsible bed and a cooker and allowed me to make morning tea without even getting out of my sleeping bag. Munday the dog accompanied us everywhere and slept beneath our bed, which was quite cosy, doggy, but cosy. The three of us motored to many places from Land's End to the Outer Hebrides, even spending one Easter on the North Yorkshire Moors where the condensation from our breath froze as icy droplets on the ceiling overnight and the water froze solid in the kettle. But we had great fun and many adventures along with Munday who always stood on the food lockers behind the front seats and always got in the way of the rear view mirror. When she suddenly died from a canine form of meningitis, it was quite a long time after before I got used to not seeing her hairy head in the rear view mirror and telling her for the trillionth time to 'Get down.' However, the wind of change was blowing and our time in Derby was coming to an end. I was determined to get back into my profession as a photographer and managed to land a job in the City Art Gallery in Manchester with its five satellite galleries. We moved and had a year in a flat before buying a 'back-to-back' house near Bacup overlooking the moors. We commuted to Manchester and Annie to her studies at a Teacher Training college. We had many adventures, got married and lived happily ever after. Well that is not entirely true of the latter, for as usual fate was once again waiting in the wings to trip me up and really go to town this time around. It seemed my destiny was to lie elsewhere and with it came a variety and richness of life with many adventures, memorable situations and unforgettable people. I suppose I should be saying here 'If only I'd known' but the thing is one never does. I strongly suspect that the not knowing is contributory to the elixir, that very essence of life which gets us all out of bed each morning in anticipation of the unknown elements of a day, along with the thought of a nice cup of tea. Speaking of which, I can think of no better time than now to put the kettle on.

If Only I'd Known!

ND - #0309 - 270225 - C0 - 234/156/12 - PB - 9781780913018 - Matt Lamination